# May Gibbs
# Needlepoint

*Designs by Alison Snepp*

🏭 BayBooks

An imprint of HarperCollins*Publishers*

# Contents

*Introduction* PAGE 3
*General instructions* PAGE 4
*Stitch instructions* PAGE 6

## Colourful Characters
*Gumnut Town library bag* PAGE 9
*Gumnut Babies cushion* PAGE 15
*Wattle Baby doll* PAGE 21
*Little Ragged Blossom doll* PAGE 25

## Subtle Distinction
*Flannel Flowers glasses case* PAGE 29
*Gumleaves workbag* PAGE 32

## Spring Blooms
*Sweet Pea glasses case* PAGE 39
*Delphinium tiebacks* PAGE 41

## Bushland
*Little Ragged Blossom box* PAGE 49
*Rambling Flowers picture* PAGE 51

## Fancy that!
*Blue & white border cushion* PAGE 55

## Pretty in Pinks
*Baby Faces doorstop* PAGE 59
*Riding Home the Dragons cushion* PAGE 61

## Midnight May
*Possum cushion* PAGE 67
*Midnight cushion* PAGE 69

## Gumleaves
*Naughty Mantis cushion* PAGE 75
*Gumleaves doorstop* PAGE 77

# *Introduction*

May Gibbs was born Cecilia May Gibbs in Surrey, England in 1877. In 1881 she emigrated to Australia with her parents and brothers. As a child she was actively encouraged by her parents to draw. Her first book, *Snugglepot and Cuddlepie*, was published in 1918 and has never been out of print. May went on to create more wonderful stories and characters which have entertained children and adults alike ever since.

Still Australia's most well-loved children's author and illustrator, her friendly bush creatures and adorable flower babies have delighted generations of Australian children. Her drawings and designs have become popular icons of Australian culture and remain a symbol of the beauty and fragility of the Australian bush.

Copyright of all May Gibbs' work rests with the Spastic Centre of New South Wales and the New South Wales Society for Children and Young Adults with Physical Disabilities and they are recipients of all royalties from the sale of this book. These beautiful projects inspired by May Gibbs' illustrations and stories are intended for personal use and not for any commercial purpose. They have been designed with the approval and co-operation of the copyright holders and their agent, Curtis Brown (Australia) Pty Ltd.

# General instructions

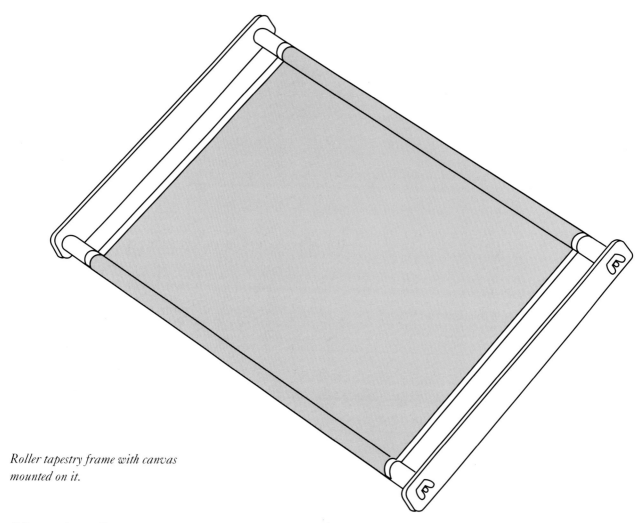

*Roller tapestry frame with canvas mounted on it.*

## Mounting the canvas onto the frame

Roller tapestry frames are available in many different varieties. Essentially a frame is made up of two fixed vertical beams, each of which holds a round 'roller' beam at each end.

There is cotton tape attached to each roller beam and the canvas is stitched onto the cotton tape.

Roller frames can be purchased from needlepoint specialist shops, craft shops and department stores. Buy a roller frame as a whole unit in a size commonly used. Later you can buy separate roller beams of various lengths as required.

The tapes on the roller beams need to be the same length as, or slightly longer than, the length of canvas to be stitched to the tapes.

After cutting a piece of tapestry canvas to the size indicated in the material requirements for each project, cover the raw edges of the canvas with masking tape. A 2 cm or 2.5 cm wide tape folded in half over these edges will stop needlepoint threads becoming snagged in the threads at the edge of the canvas.

Find the centre of the two opposite edges of the canvas which will be attached to the roller beams. Find the centre of the cotton tapes attached to the roller beams. Mark the centres with a stitch or an indelible pen. Match the centre mark on the canvas with the centre mark on the tape and stitch the canvas to the tape. Use a running stitch — it doesn't have to be tiny, 1 cm long stitches are fine — with a strong thread or wool threaded onto a chenille needle to make the job easier.

Attach the other end of the canvas to the tape on the other roller beam in the same manner. Before stitching the second end of the canvas to the second beam, check that the canvas is facing the right direction (refer to illustration).

Wind the canvas around the beams so that the middle of the canvas or the top of the canvas is visible between the beams, according to the instructions for the project to be stitched.

The canvas will be easier to stitch if it is drum tight on the frame. Lace the edges of the canvas to the side beams on the roller frame and tighten the lacings so that the canvas is drum tight. These lacings may have to be tightened periodically to maintain the tension of the canvas.

When the needlepoint on an area of canvas between the beams is complete, untie the lacings, wind the canvas on around a roller beam and replace the lacings before beginning the next section of needlepoint.

## To end off

To end off needlepoint stitches, push the needle under six stitches on the back of the work and clip the thread off close to the needlepoint. Don't leave tags of thread on the wrong side of the work.

HINT: Don't jump more than three or four stitches from one area of colour to another area of the same colour. It is better to end off and start again by running under the stitches at the back of the work.

## Blocking instructions

Blocking is the process which straightens crooked canvas, stretches out any minor irregularities in the needlepoint and firms the canvas which is likely to have softened while it was being stitched. Always block a piece of needlepoint as a square or rectangle (that is, before cutting it out).

You will need a flat square or rectangular piece of wood which is 10 cm or more larger than the canvas on all sides. Particle board is not suitable as it is too hard; cork is too soft.

You will also need some 20–25 mm nails, a hammer and a water spray. After the stitched canvas has been taken from the frame, spray the back of it with cold water from the water spray. Don't saturate the canvas, but it should be wet. Place the canvas right side down onto the blocking board.

Nail two adjacent sides of the canvas to the board, keeping the edges of the canvas parallel with the edges of the board. Don't hammer the nails in far — four or five firm taps will do.

Nail the other two sides of the canvas to the board, pulling the canvas very tightly before hammering in the nails. The canvas should be nailed out square and as tight as possible onto the board. Leave the canvas in an airy place out of the sun to dry thoroughly. If you like, you can then leave the dry canvas on the board in a dry place until you are ready to make up the project. Specialist needlework shops and framers usually offer a blocking service if you don't want to brave hammer and nails yourself!

# Stitch instructions

The designs in this book are shown in chart form. One square on the chart represents one stitch on the canvas. Each symbol shown within each square on a chart represents a colour. Refer to a chart's key to see which colour is represented by which symbol.

Where other stitches are used in some charts, they are noted in the instructions and the key to the appropriate chart.

## Continental Stitch

Each Continental Stitch covers one intersection of canvas and lies in an oblique direction sloping from lower left to top right.

When working a row from right to left, bring the needle up through the canvas at 1, count over and up one thread and push the needle back down through the canvas at 2. Bring the needle up through the canvas at 3, down at 4 and so on.

When working from left to right, turn the stitch illustration upside down and follow 1, 2, 3, 4, etc. Work each stitch in two separate movements – push the needle down through the canvas and gently pull the stitch into position. Then push the needle back up through the canvas and, again, pull the thread through into position ready for the next stitch.

The back of the work should show a long sloping stitch, except when changing rows. This needlepoint stitch should always be worked on a frame, otherwise it distorts the canvas badly and blocking may not correct the distortion.

## Basketweave Stitch

Basketweave Stitch is an excellent needlepoint stitch for covering large areas of canvas such as backgrounds. It is worked in diagonal rows on the canvas. It is easy to work and does not distort the canvas when worked correctly.

When starting from a corner of the canvas, follow the sequence of numbers shown in the stitch illustration. Once three or four rows have been worked, you will see that when stitching up a diagonal row the stitch on the back of the work will be horizontal, and when stitching down the next diagonal row the stitch on the back of the work will be vertical. This is important to remember when starting in a new section of work. The highlighted areas on the stitch diagram will help to locate vertical and horizontal rows.

Take care to count the needle positions carefully when changing rows until you are confident about the turning sequence.

HINT: End off a thread in the middle of a row where possible, as it will be easy to see if you are on an up row or a down row when stitching in that area again.

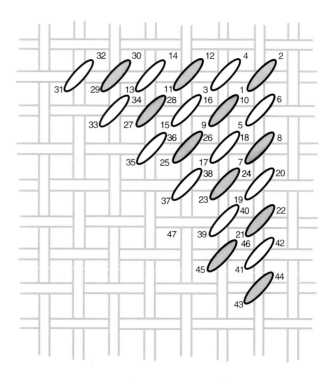

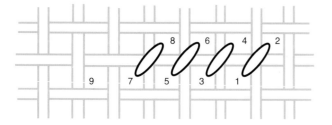

## French Knot

French Knots are dotted around in several of the designs in the book. They are drawn onto the charts with separate symbols which appear in the keys. Always work the French Knots in these designs after the needlepoint has been completed.

Bring the threaded needle up through the canvas where the knot is to lie. Point the needle up and twist the thread once or twice around the needle. Put the needle down into the fabric over or between needlepoint stitches, at the same time pulling the knot firmly around the needle.

Hold the knot while pulling the needle through to the back of the needlepoint.

## Back Stitch

Back Stitch is used for outline detail in most of the designs in the book. The key for each chart will show which colour and thread to use, as well as how many strands.

Some of the Back Stitches are worked over needlepoint stitches and others are worked between them — the chart will show where to place the stitches. The Back Stitches may be worked over one thread of canvas or over two or more threads. Work eyelashes as one long Back Stitch. Work outlines over or between one or two needlepoint stitches.

Follow the figure to see an example of the direction of the stitches and how to make them.

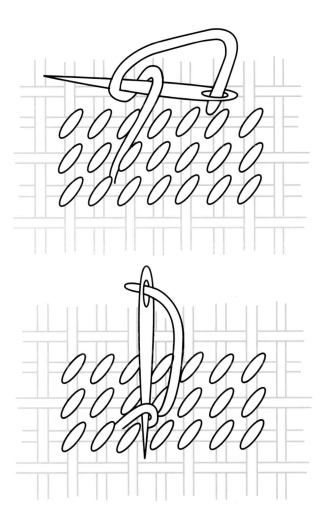

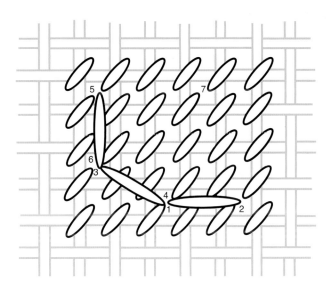

Background fabric from Wardlaw

# Colourful Characters

## Gumnut Town library bag

### Materials

DMC Tapestry Wool (Art. 486) in the following colours and skein quantities:

| | | | |
|---|---|---|---|
| 7107 | 1 | 7510 | 1 |
| 7122 | 1 | 7587 | 3 |
| 7123 | 1 | 7593 | 1 |
| 7175 | 2 | 7618 | 1 |
| 7200 | 1 | 7701 | 1 |
| 7215 | 1 | 7702 | 6 |
| 7266 | 2 | 7725 | 2 |
| 7283 | 1 | 7760 | 1 |
| 7298 | 4 | 7840 | 2 |
| 7304 | 5 | 7912 | 1 |
| 7337 | 1 | 7949 | 2 |
| 7370 | 1 | black | 2 |
| 7466 | 2 | ecru | 3 |
| 7491 | 1 | | |

DMC Stranded Cotton (Art. 117), 1 skein 839
Zweigart Tapestry Canvas (Art. 604–48), 42 x 58 cm
Tapestry needle, size 22
Embroidery scissors
Roller tapestry frame
1.3 m medium-weight cotton fabric, blue
Machine cotton to match
50 cm medium-weight interfacing (not iron-on)

Mount the tapestry canvas onto the roller frame. The short ends of the canvas should be sewn onto the tapes on the frame. Measure 6 cm in and 6 cm down from the top left hand corner of the canvas. This point corresponds to the top left hand corner of the chart. Start the needlepoint here. The needlepoint should be worked in Continental Stitch. Work the Back Stitch details after the Continental Stitch is complete.
Block the finished needlepoint.
Cut out the needlepoint, leaving 2 cm of unworked canvas all around it.
Cut a piece of blue backing fabric for the back of the library bag, making it the same size as the canvas. Cut a length of blue fabric 7 cm x 1.25 m for the gusset. Cut two pieces of blue fabric each 12 x 36 cm for the handles. For the lining, cut two more pieces the size of the back of the bag and another piece the same size as the gusset.
From the interfacing fabric cut three

# CHART 1

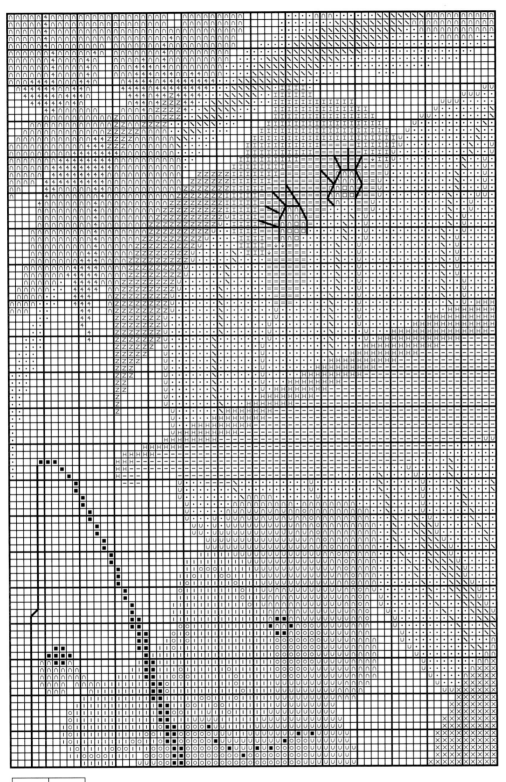

**KEY**

⊞ 7122 very light salmon pink
⊟ 7725 topaz
⌂ ecru
⊠ 7491 very light rose beige
☒ 7337 medium midnight blue
◉ 7681 very light acid yellow
■ black
⊍ 7840 medium negro flesh
⊠ 7123 salmon pink
⊙ 7466 medium forest brown
Ⅰ 7175 light orange
Ⅵ 7510 very light grey sand
⊟ 7200 ultra very light dusty rose
↧ 7215 medium salmon pink
⊡ 7283 mid blue
▶ 7370 light tartan green
Ⅱ 7912 light jade
Ⅳ 7701 dark blue green
⊡ 7702 medium blue green
☑ 7107 bright red
⊞ 7760 salmon
☑ 7593 very light greyed blue
⊞ 7587 palest blue
⊡ 7298 light blue
⊤ 7949 chocolate brown
☒ 7266 medium antique violet
☐ 7304 medium baby blue
◟ black back stitch for fishing line – use full thickness of wool
◟ 839 brown – back stitch for eyes and eyelashes – use 2 strands

# CHART 2

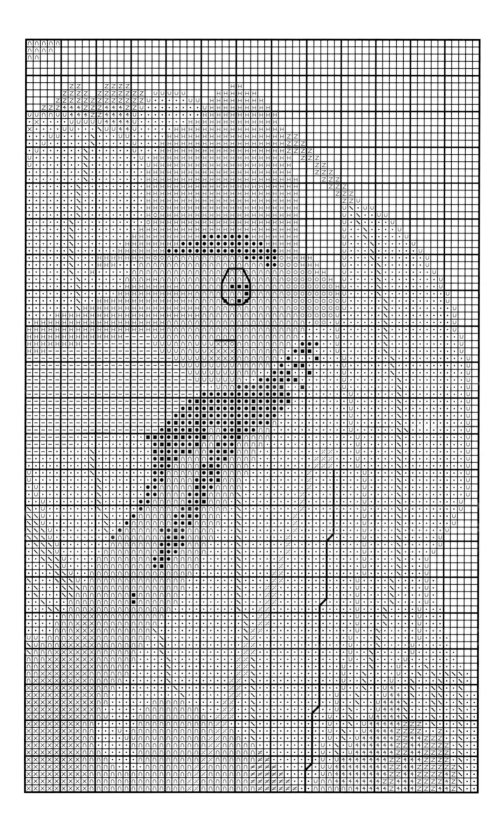

# CHART 3

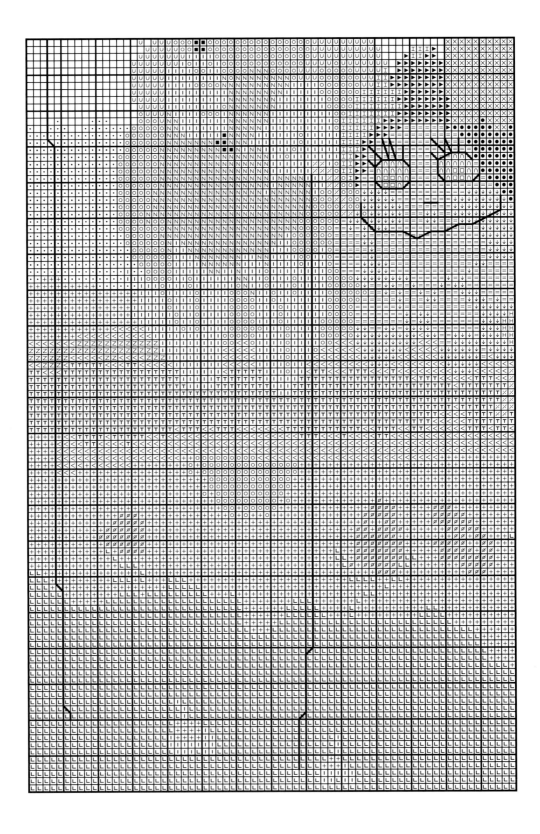

# CHART 4

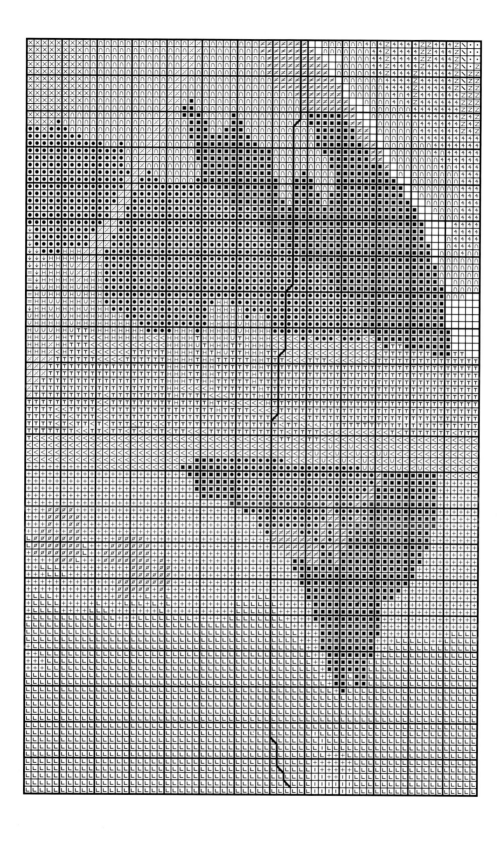

pieces: one the size of the front of the bag, one the size of the back of the bag and one the size of the gusset.

Tack a piece of interfacing to the back of the tapestry, the back of the lining and the back of the gusset.

Tack a line across the gusset 40 cm in from each end. These lines mark the corners of the bag.

Pin and tack the gusset to the front of the bag with right sides together, snipping the seam allowances at the corners to allow the gusset to be turned.

Pin the other side of the gusset to the back of the bag with right sides together, taking care to match the tacking lines to the corners. Clip the seam allowances to allow the corners to be turned.

Machine stitch the bag together, reinforcing the corners with extra stitching.

Assemble the lining of the bag in the same manner, but without interfacing.

### HANDLES

Fold each long side of a handle section to the middle of the strip. Pin it into position. Fold the handle in half again and pin it. Repeat with the other handle. Each handle will now be 3 cm wide x 36 cm long. Machine stitch all around the handles close to the edge.

Place an end of each handle 7 cm in from each bag/gusset seam, making one handle on each side of the bag. Machine stitch the handles firmly into position close to the top of the bag.

Turn back the top seam allowance around the top of the bag, making sure that the handles protrude from the top of the bag. Turn top of lining to wrong side and tack back.

Place lining into the bag with wrong sides facing, making sure that the gusset seams and the top edges match.

Pin and machine stitch all around the top of the bag close to the edge, with the outside of the bag uppermost. The stitching should be between the first and second row of needlepoint stitches.

# Gumnut Babies cushion

## Materials

DMC Tapestry Wool (Art. 486) in the following colours and skein quantities:

| | | | |
|------|----|------|----|
| 7107 | 1  | 7448 | 1  |
| 7108 | 1  | 7451 | 18 |
| 7120 | 1  | 7460 | 4  |
| 7121 | 2  | 7538 | 1  |
| 7215 | 1  | 7725 | 1  |
| 7241 | 1  | 7727 | 1  |
| 7243 | 1  | 7759 | 1  |
| 7301 | 1  | 7760 | 1  |
| 7323 | 1  | 7802 | 1  |
| 7372 | 1  | 7853 | 2  |
| 7392 | 1  | 7922 | 1  |
| 7417 | 1  | ecru | 1  |
| 7446 | 1  | | |

Zweigart Tapestry Canvas (Art. 604–48),
40 x 40 cm
Tapestry needle, size 22
Embroidery scissors
Roller tapestry frame
40 cm medium-weight cotton fabric,
apricot
Machine cotton to match
30 x 30 cm cushion insert
1.4 m cotton piping cord

Mount the tapestry canvas onto the roller frame.

Measure 17 cm in from the left edge of the canvas and 7 cm down from the top edge of the canvas and mark the spot with a pin. Locate the top stitch on the hat of the Christmas Bell Baby (which is the top left baby in the design). Work the top stitch on the hat at the spot marked with a pin and continue the needlepoint from there. Work the design in Continental Stitch.

The background extends to the edge of the chart and should be worked in Basketweave Stitch.

Work the Back Stitch detail for the eyelashes, mouths and noses with a full strand of wool in the colour shown in the key. Remove the canvas from the frame and block it.

From the apricot fabric cut a square of backing fabric 40 x 40 cm. From the remaining fabric cut 1.4 m bias following the instructions shown in figure i on page 20. Join the bias strips following figure ii and machine stitch as shown. Press the seams open.

Fold the bias strip around the piping cord as shown in figure iii and pin the cord into position. Place the zipper foot onto the sewing machine and straight stitch close to the cord.

Pin the piping to the needlepoint one row in from the edge, starting halfway along the bottom edge of the design. The raw edge of the piping should face towards the outside edge of the canvas. Clip the seam allowances on the piping several times when attaching it to the corners, at the same time gently curve the piping around the corners. Pin the piping all around the cushion until the starting point is reached. Unpick a little stitching in the piping and join the two ends of the bias so they fit smoothly onto the cushion. Trim the seam allowances. Place the cord back into the bias, overlapping the ends of the cord in the channel as shown in figure iv on page 20. Machine stitch the join close to the cord, keeping the piping free of the needlepoint. Pin the rest of the piping into place.

NOTE: The piping should be attached one row in from the edge of the needlepoint all around the cushion so that unstitched canvas will not show at the edge of the cushion.

Machine stitch the piping to the needlepoint, stitching close to the outer edge of the cord with the zipper foot on the sewing machine.

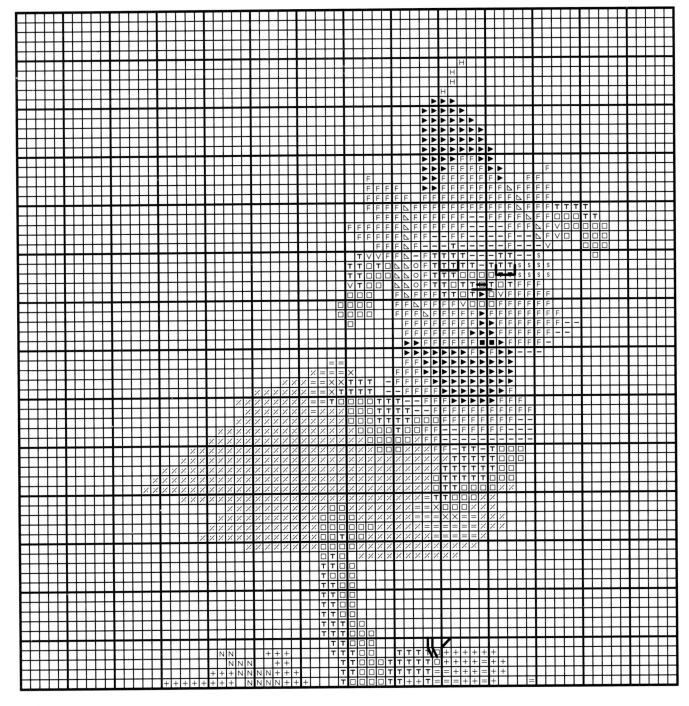

## KEY

| | | | | | | |
|---|---|---|---|---|---|---|
| ⊡ | 7727 | very light topaz | ☑ | 7301 | very light electric blue | |
| ⑤ | 7725 | topaz | ⊞ | 7243 | violet | |
| ◼ | 7538 | very dark brownish green | ☒ | 7241 | greyed mauve | |
| ◺ | 7446 | dark orange | ⊞ | 7108 | red | |
| ⊠ | 7392 | light fern green | ⊟ | 7759 | medium salmon | |
| ☑ | 7417 | very dark lime green | Ⅳ | 7760 | salmon | |
| ⊡ | 7448 | very dark rose brown | Ⅎ | 7922 | bright mahogany | |
| ◉ | 7372 | ultra very dark wine red | ▶ | 7107 | bright red | |
| ◹ | 7323 | light grey green | ⊡ | 7121 | light peach flesh | |
| ⊤ | 7802 | baby blue | ⊤ | 7853 | peach flesh | |

| | | |
|---|---|---|
| ☑ | 7120 | very pale grey mauve |
| ⊙ | ecru | |
| ☑ | 7460 | ultra very light beige brown |
| ☐ | 7451 | ultra very light antique mauve for background |
| ⌐ | 7215 | medium salmon pink |

# CHART 2

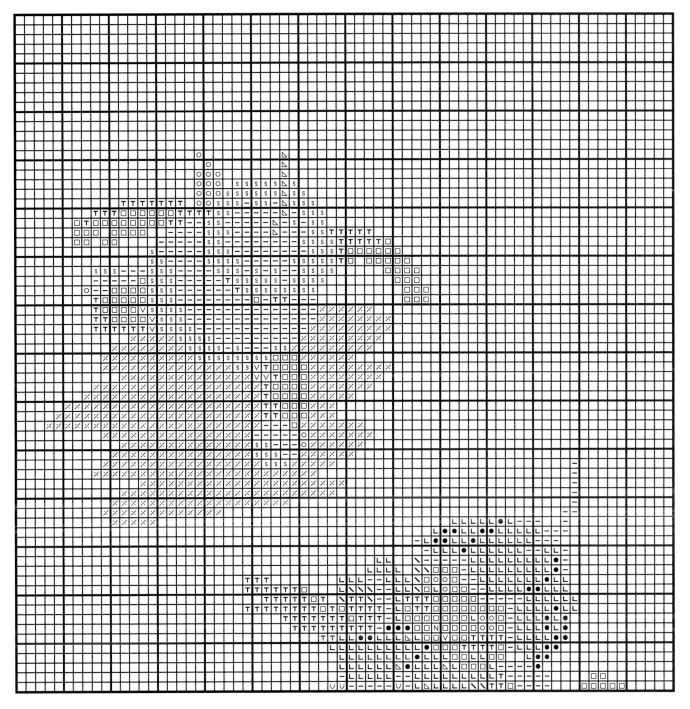

## CHART 3

## CHART 4

Press the backing fabric and place it on top of the piped needlepoint, with right sides together. Pin the backing fabric into position close to the outer edge of the piping. Machine stitch the backing to the needlepoint on the outside of the piping cord, close to the piping cord, using the zipper foot on the sewing machine. On the bottom edge of the cushion, stitch only 3 cm around each corner, leaving a large gap unstitched. This gap is to turn the cushion and to insert the cushion filling.

Trim the seam allowances to 1 cm from the stitching and zigzag the raw edges of the cushion, taking care to zigzag each side of the gap in the lower edge of the cushion. Turn the cushion right side out. Push out the corners from the inside of the cushion. Place the insert into the cushion and slip stitch the opening closed.

Most specialist needlework shops offer a finishing service and they will arrange to have your cushion blocked and made up for you.

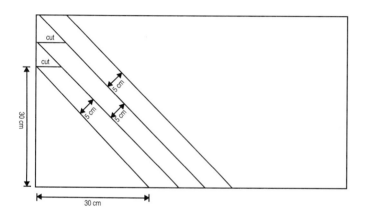

i *Cut bias for piping*

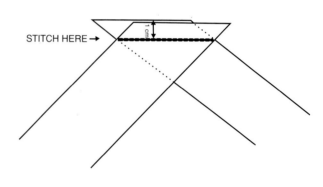

ii *Join bias strips*

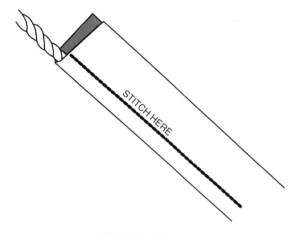

iii *Stitch piping*

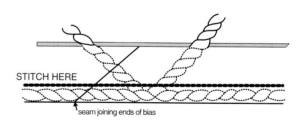

iv *Overlap the ends of the cord in the bias to join cord*

# *Wattle Baby doll*

*Materials*

DMC Tapestry Wool (Art. 486) in the following colours and skein quantities:

| | | | |
|---|---|---|---|
| 7108 | 1 | 7426 | 3 |
| 7121 | 5 | 7467 | 3 |
| 7191 | 4 | 7504 | 9 |
| 7195 | 1 | 7725 | 3 |
| 7302 | 1 | 7727 | 4 |
| 7361 | 1 | 7853 | 2 |
| 7377 | 3 | ecru | 1 |

DMC Stranded Cotton (Art. 117), 1 skein 3773
Zweigart Tapestry Canvas (Art. 604–48), 32 x 45 cm
Tapestry needle, size 22
Embroidery scissors
Roller tapestry frame
30 cm medium-weight cotton fabric, green
Machine cotton to match
Polyester cushion filling

Mount the short ends of the canvas onto the roller frame.

Find the centre stitch on the lower edge of the chart for the top half of the doll. Find the centre of the canvas and mark this spot with a pin. These two points (the centre stitch and the centre of the canvas) correspond. Start the needlepoint here. Work the design in Continental Stitch. After the Continental Stitch is complete, work the Back Stitch detail on the feet, using two strands of stranded cotton. Remove the canvas from the frame and block it.

Cut a piece of backing fabric which is 30 x 45 cm and press it. Place the needlepoint and the backing fabric together with right sides facing. Pin them together around the outside of the doll shape and machine stitch the two layers together one row in from the edge of the needlepoint, evening out corners to a smooth sweep where necessary. Leave an unstitched gap about 10 cm long along the straightest part of the design (the edge on the left beside the left leg). Machine stitch around the doll again for strength, stitching just outside the original stitching.

Trim seam allowances to 1 cm from machine stitching. Zigzag around the cut edges, making sure to zigzag each side of the opening separately. Clip the curves of the canvas. Turn the doll right side out and fill her with polyester cushion filling. Slip stitch the opening closed.

**CHART 1**

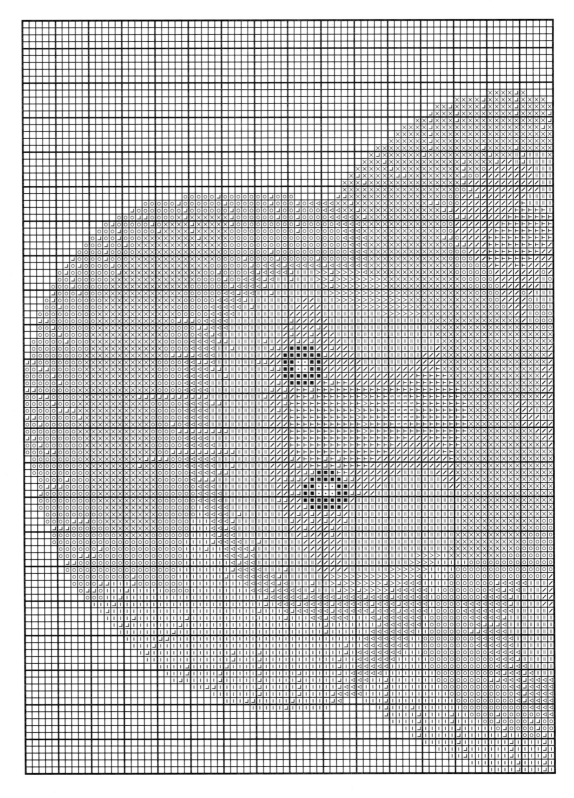

**KEY**

| | | |
|---|---|---|
| ☒ 7727 very light topaz | ▣ 7302 light baby blue | ☑ 7195 medium shell pink |
| ◙ 7504 light golden olive | ⊡ ecru | ⑤ 7108 red |
| ⊟ 7725 topaz | ⊑ 7467 forest brown | ⌐ 3773 dark skin pink (Art. 117) |
| ▣ 7377 dark eucalyptus green | ⊤ 7191 very light peach flesh | for outlines – |
| ⊡ 7426 medium eucalyptus green | ⊠ 7121 light peach flesh | use 2 strands |
| ⊿ 7361 very light lime green | ☐ 7853 peach flesh | |

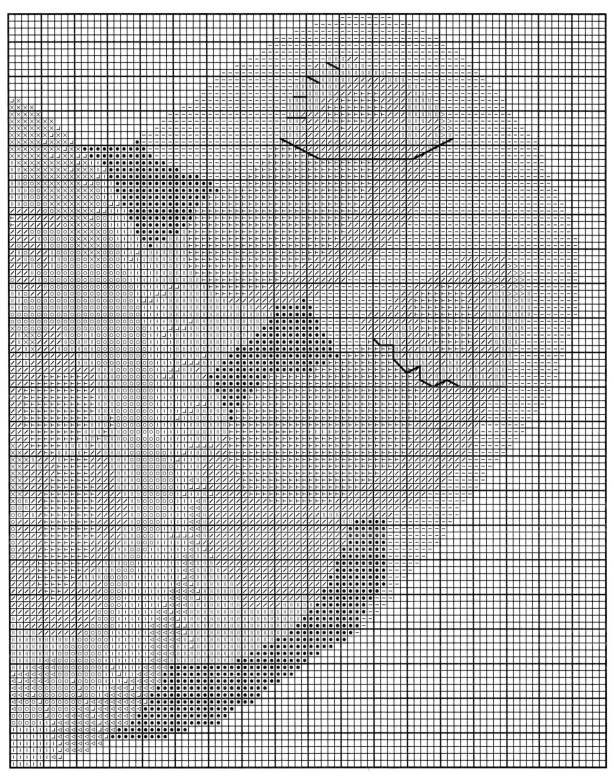

**CHART 2**

# Little Ragged Blossom doll

## Materials

DMC Tapestry Wool (Art. 486) in the following colours and skein quantities:

| | | | |
|------|---|------|---|
| 7121 | 1 | 7470 | 2 |
| 7215 | 1 | 7491 | 1 |
| 7304 | 1 | 7492 | 1 |
| 7326 | 1 | 7493 | 1 |
| 7361 | 2 | 7853 | 2 |
| 7377 | 1 | ecru | 1 |
| 7426 | 1 | | |

DMC Stranded Cotton (Art. 117), 1 skein
838
Zweigart Tapestry Canvas (Art. 604–48),
20 x 38 cm
Tapestry needle, size 22
Embroidery scissors
Roller tapestry frame
Medium-weight cotton fabric, ecru,
20 x 40 cm
Machine cotton to match
Polyester blending machine thread, clear
Polyester cushion filling
Straw needle, size 4

Mount the canvas onto the roller frame. Start the needlepoint at the top of the design in the centre of the top row of the baby's hat. Start stitching 5 cm down from the top of the canvas using Continental Stitch.

When the needlepoint is complete, embroider the eyelashes with one strand of 838. Each eyelash is one stitch.

Finally, embroider the French Knots with a full thickness of the tapestry wool in ecru. Remove the needlepoint from the roller frame and block it.

Cut out the doll shape 1 cm outside the outer edge of needlepoint. Turn back the unworked margin of canvas behind the needlepoint so that no unworked canvas can be seen. Clip the curves where necessary. Pin in position.

Thread the straw needle with a doubled length of clear polyester machine thread and knot the two ends of the thread together. Stitch between every second or third needlepoint stitch to hold the turned-back seam allowance in position behind the needlepoint. Cut out a doll shape, adding a 1 cm seam allowance all around, from the ecru cotton backing fabric. Put the backing fabric and the needlepoint together with wrong sides facing. Turn back the seam allowances on the backing fabric, clipping them where necessary, so that the backing fabric lies neatly behind the needlepoint.

Slip stitch the backing into place around the edge of the needlepoint. Leave a gap for stuffing the doll along the lower edge of the needlepoint. Fill the doll firmly with polyester cushion filling — a chopstick may be useful to help push the filling into the doll.

Slip stitch the opening closed.

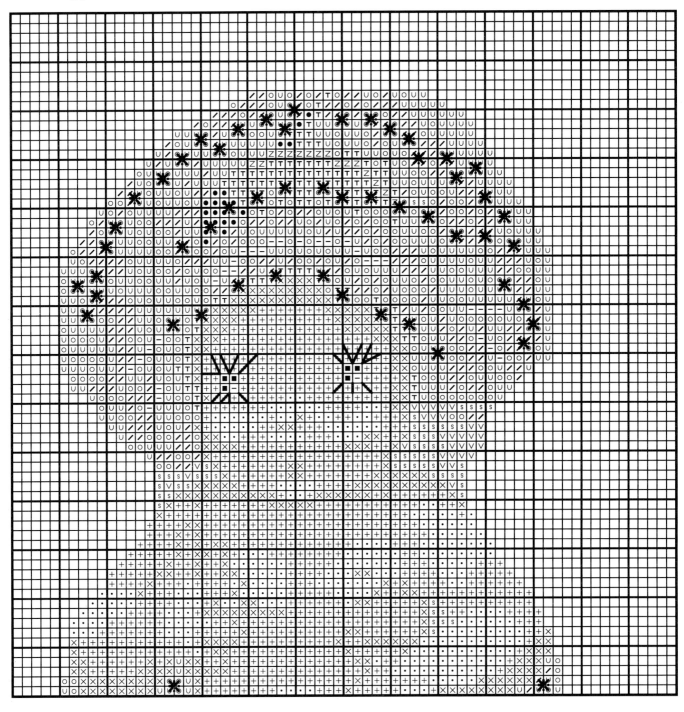

## CHART 1

### KEY

- ■ 7304  medium baby blue
- ⊠ 7215  medium salmon pink
- ⊡ 7121  light peach flesh
- ⊞ 7853  peach flesh
- ⊟ ecru

- ⊡ 7470  ultra very light avocado green
- ⊠ 7493  light sand
- ⊔ 7361  very light lime green
- Ⅎ 7426  medium eucalyptus green
- ⊠ 7326  aqua marine
- ◉ 7377  dark eucalyptus green

- ⊠ 7491  very light rose beige
- ⊠ 7492  very light drab brown
- ⭦ 838  brown (Art. 117) for back stitch on eyelashes – use 1 strand
- ✷ ecru for french knots – use full thickness of wool

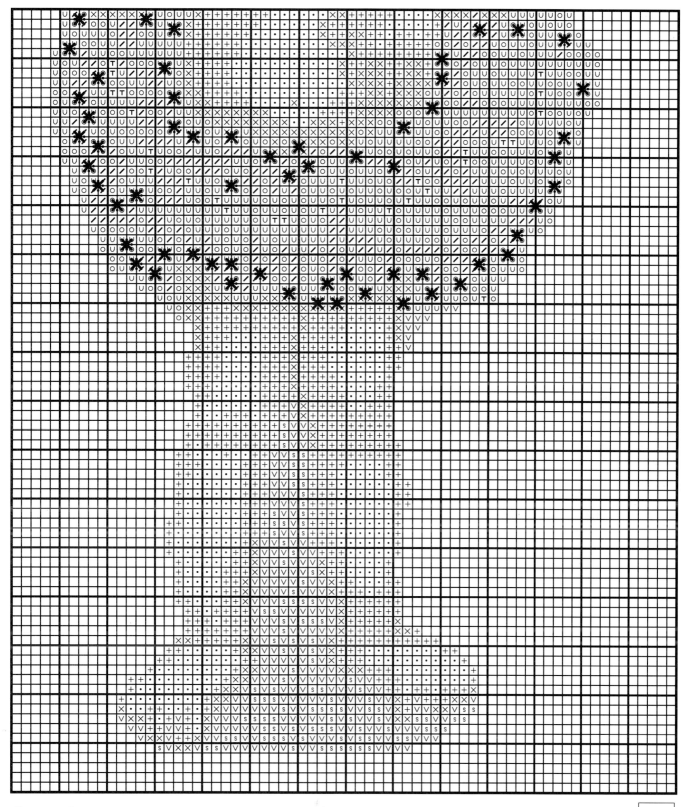

**CHART 2**

# Subtle Distinction

## Flannel Flowers glasses case

### Materials

DMC Tapestry Wool (Art. 486) in the following colours and skein quantities:

| | | | |
|---|---|---|---|
| 7170 | 1 | 7510 | 5 |
| 7215 | 1 | 7523 | 3 |
| 7370 | 1 | 7587 | 1 |
| 7400 | 1 | 7758 | 1 |
| 7416 | 1 | 7870 | 3 |
| 7470 | 1 | ecru | 5 |

Zweigart Tapestry Canvas (Art. 604–48), 32 x 32 cm
Tapestry needle, size 22
Embroidery scissors
Roller tapestry frame
20 cm medium-weight fabric, pale green
Machine cotton to match
Machine cotton to match background colour of needlepoint
Polyester blending machine thread, clear
Straw needle, size 4

Fold the canvas in half and tack a line down the centre fold. The Flannel Flower design will be worked twice — once into each half of the canvas.
Mount the canvas onto the roller frame.

Find the centre of one half of the canvas and the centre of the Flannel Flower pattern chart. These points correspond. Start the needlepoint in the centre of the design. Work the design in Continental Stitch and the background in Basketweave Stitch. When the design is complete, work the same design into the second half of the canvas.
Remove the canvas from the frame and block it.
Cut out each side of the glasses case, leaving 1 cm of unworked canvas around the outside.
Turn back and pin the unworked margin of canvas behind the needlepoint, carefully easing in the fullness around the corners. Thread the straw needle with a double thickness of polyester blending thread, knot the two ends together and stitch the seam allowance back by taking a stitch between every third or fourth needlepoint stitch. Repeat this procedure for the second half of the glasses case.
From the green lining fabric cut two pieces, each 11 x 20 cm. Place one lining section

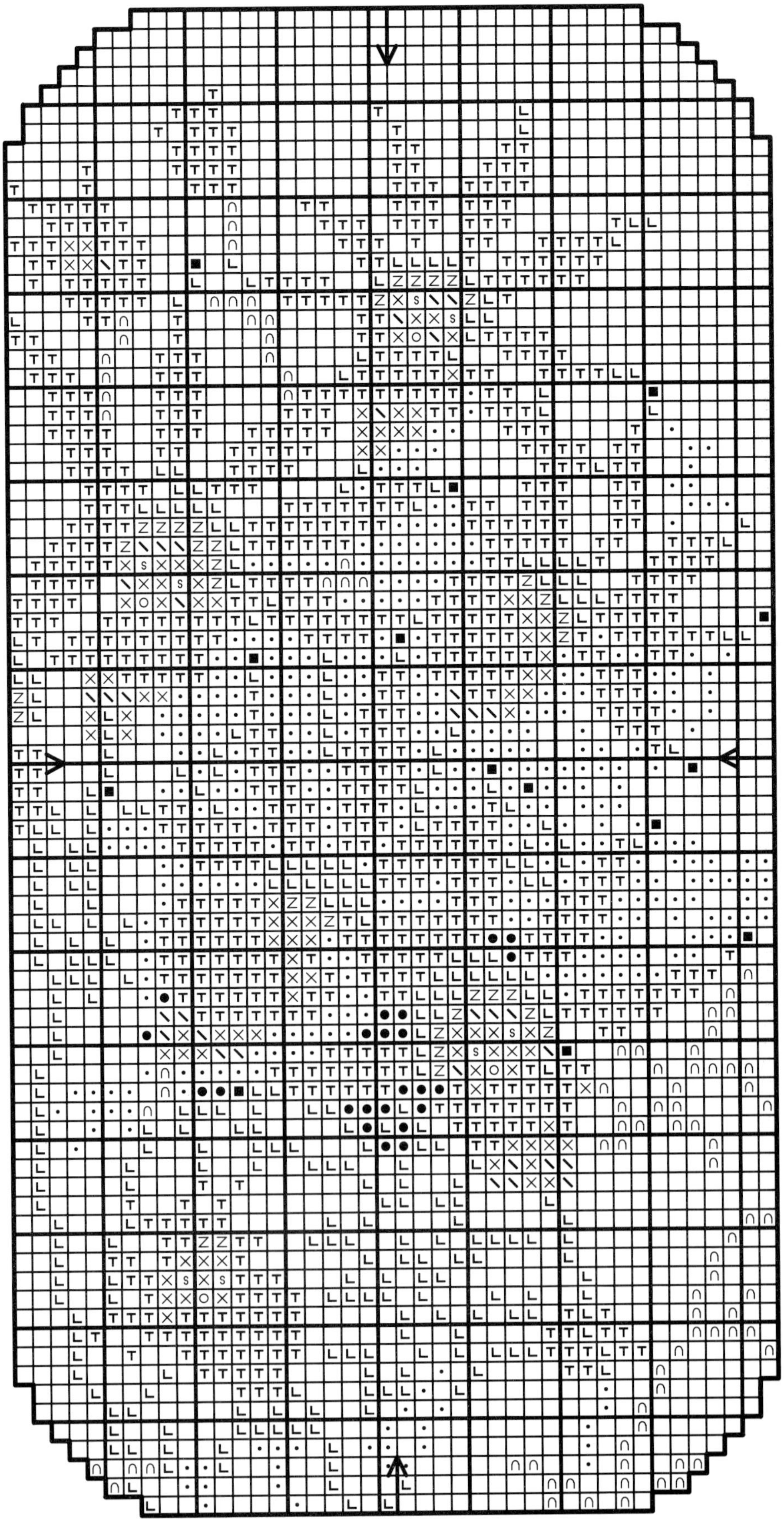

**KEY**

- ▣ 7370 light tartan green
- L 7870 very light fern green
- ∩ 7400 ultra very light bush green
- T ecru
- □ 7510 very light grey sand
- · 7523 very light sandy brown
- • 7416 dark drab brown
- s 7587 palest blue
- \ 7215 medium salmon pink
- X 7170 pinkish white
- Z 7470 ultra very light avocado green
- O 7758 dark salmon

behind each needlepoint section with wrong sides facing. Turn back the seam allowances on the lining to fit the back of the needlepoint so that no unworked canvas is visible. Slip stitch the lining to the edge of the needlepoint.

### TWISTED CORD

Cut four 1.85 m lengths of 7870. Tie the four ends together at one end and close the knot in a tightly-fitting drawer. Stand at the other end of the threads and twist them together (in the same direction as the twist in the wool) until they are tightly twisted. Taking care not to allow the threads to become tangled, tie the end which was being twisted to the knot in the drawer and allow the cord to twist up on itself to form a well-twisted cord.

Place the two sections of the glasses case together with the lined sides innermost and pin them together around the outside. Thread the straw needle with a doubled-double length (i.e. four thicknesses) of machine cotton to match the background of the needlepoint.

Sew the two sides of the glasses case together, starting just below the bottom of the curve at the top of the case and stitch down the side, across the bottom edge and up the other side, finishing at the bottom end of the curve on the second side. The top of the glasses case will remain open. Thread the straw needle with a single strand of machine cotton to match the twisted cord. Push the folded end of the twisted cord inside the glasses case where the stitching joining the two sides began. Ensure that the folded end is pushed as close as possible into the seam inside the glasses case. Stitch the cord to the outer edge of the glasses case, moving first up around one side of the top opening in the case, down the side, across the bottom, up the other side and across the other side of the top opening. Tie a knot in the cord where its end will be pushed inside the seam, cut off any excess cord beyond the knot and push the knot into the seam. Finish stitching the cord to the edge of the glasses case.

HINT: Don't cut the cord before tying a knot, otherwise it will become untwisted.

# Gumleaves workbag

*Materials*

DMC Tapestry Wool (Art. 486) in the following colours and skein quantities:

| | |
|---|---|
| 7170 | 38 |
| 7870 | 22 |

Zweigart Tapestry Canvas (Art. 604–48), a piece 55 x 40 cm and a piece 28 x 38 cm

Tapestry needle, size 22

Embroidery scissors

Roller tapestry frame

1 m medium-weight cotton fabric to match background colour

Machine cotton to match

50 cm medium-weight interfacing (not iron-on)

Polyester blending machine thread, clear

20 x 40 cm heavy cardboard or strawboard

Strong thread or wool for lacing

2 m thick cotton tape or braid (1.5 cm wide) to match background colour

1 brass ring or split ring (1.5 cm diameter)

Straw needle, size 3

Find the centre of the larger tapestry canvas and tack centre lines horizontally and vertically across the canvas. Mount the long sides of the larger piece of tapestry canvas onto the roller frame. Start the needlepoint at the centre of the canvas, taking care to align the rectangular shape of the chart with the rectangular shape of the canvas.

First work the gum leaf lines in Continental Stitch, then the background in Basketweave Stitch.

When the needlepoint is complete, remove it from the frame and mount the smaller piece of canvas. Find the centre of the long edge of the canvas and tack a centre line. Work one circular end panel into the centre of each half of the canvas. Work the Continental Stitch leaf lines first, then the background in Basketweave Stitch. Remove the canvas from the frame and block each piece of needlepoint.

Cut out the large rectangle of needlepoint, leaving a seam allowance of 1.5 cm of unworked canvas on all sides.

Cut out a piece of interfacing slightly smaller than the area of the needlepoint on the rectangular canvas. Pin the interfacing to the wrong side of the needlepoint and slip stitch around the outside.

Turn back the seam allowances towards the wrong side of the needlepoint so that no unworked canvas is visible. Fold in a mitre at the corners. Pin back the seam allowances all around. Thread the straw needle with a doubled length of the clear polyester blending thread and knot the cut ends together. Stitch back the seam allowances on the canvas by taking a stitch through the canvas and seam allowances from the right side every three or four needlepoint stitches. These stitches should be pulled fairly firmly so that they disappear between the needlepoint stitches.

Cut a piece of lining fabric which is the width of the shorter side of the needlepoint plus 3 cm seam allowance, by the length of the long side of the needlepoint (don't add any seam allowances). Place the embroidered canvas into the middle of the lining fabric with wrong sides together. Turn in the seam allowances to fit along the long edges of the lining. Along the short edges of the lining turn in a seam allowance of 1.5 cm at each end. This will mean that the lining is shorter than the needlepoint. Pin the short ends of the lining with their turned-back seam allowances to the short ends of the canvas. Spread the lining down the length of the needlepoint so that the lining is spaced evenly down the length of the canvas. The canvas should bow upwards to form a slight U-shape.

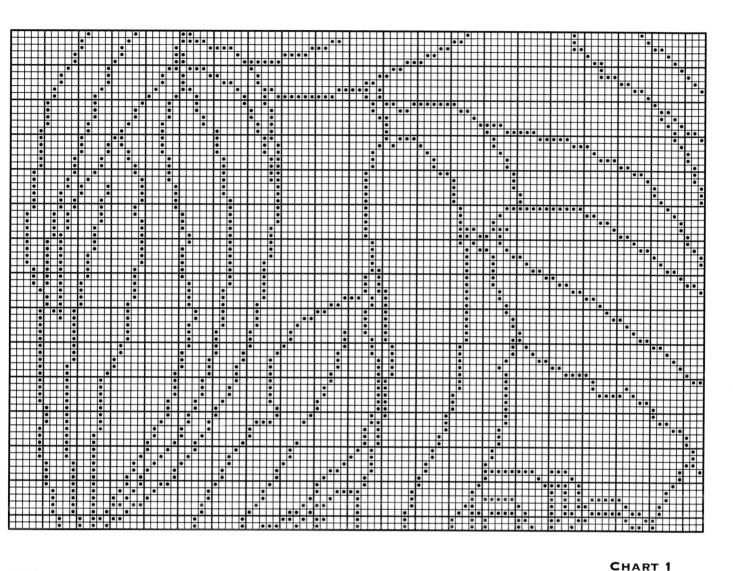

**KEY**

☐ 7870  very light fern green

◻ 7170  pinkish white for background

**CHART 1**

Slip stitch the lining to the edge of the canvas, using a doubled thickness of matching machine thread.

Cut two circles each 9.7 cm diameter from the cardboard. Cut out each of the circular needlepoint sections from the canvas, leaving a 1.5 cm seam allowance all around each piece.

Place a cardboard circle on the wrong side of each needlepoint circle and lace the needlepoint around the cardboard using the strong thread or wool. Put in enough lacings to ease in the fullness of the seam allowance.

Cut two circles of lining fabric, each the size of the laced needlepoint sections plus 1.5 cm seam allowance. Place the lining and the laced section with wrong sides together. Turn in the seam allowances on the lining to fit, and pin the lining to the back of the laced section so that no unworked canvas can be seen. Slip stitch the lining into position.

Pin a lined end section to the corner of a

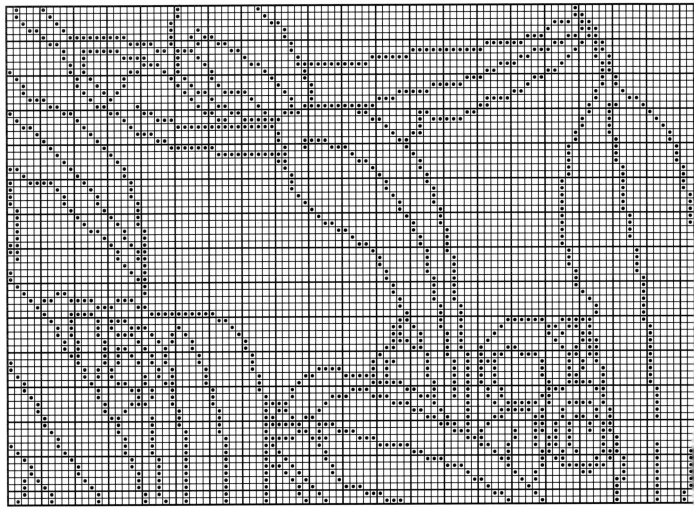

**CHART 2**

long side of the body of the workbag. Pin the long side of the rectangular needlepoint about three quarters of the way around the end section. Pin the other end section to the other long side of the body of the workbag in a corresponding manner. HINT: Check that the leaf design in the needlepoint is facing down on both end sections.

Stitch the ends to the body of the bag using a doubled-double length (i.e. four thicknesses) of matching machine thread in the straw needle.

Wrap the thick cotton braid around the workbag following the illustration on page 37 to form the handles of the workbag. Stitch each handle from A to B only. Cover the brass or split ring with 7170 and attach it to the bag below the flap. Make a loop with 7170 on the edge of the flap to fit the covered ring.

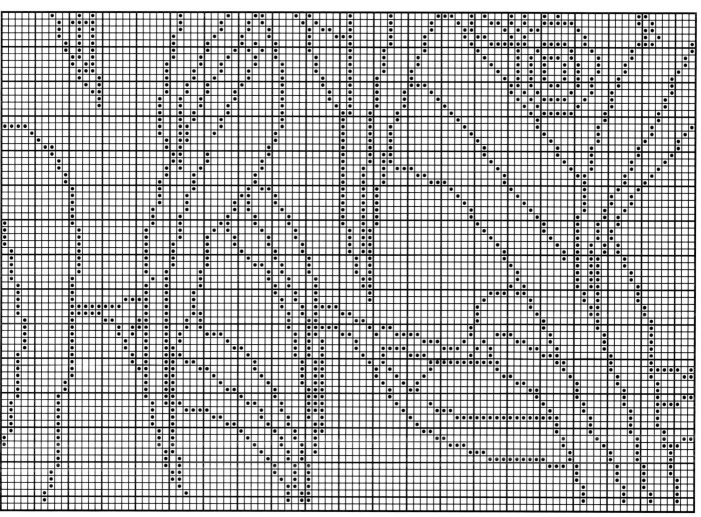

**CHART 3**

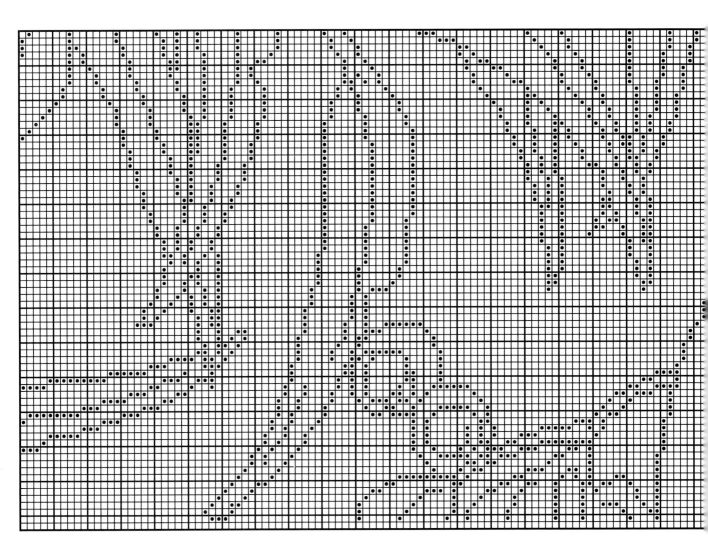

**CHART 4**

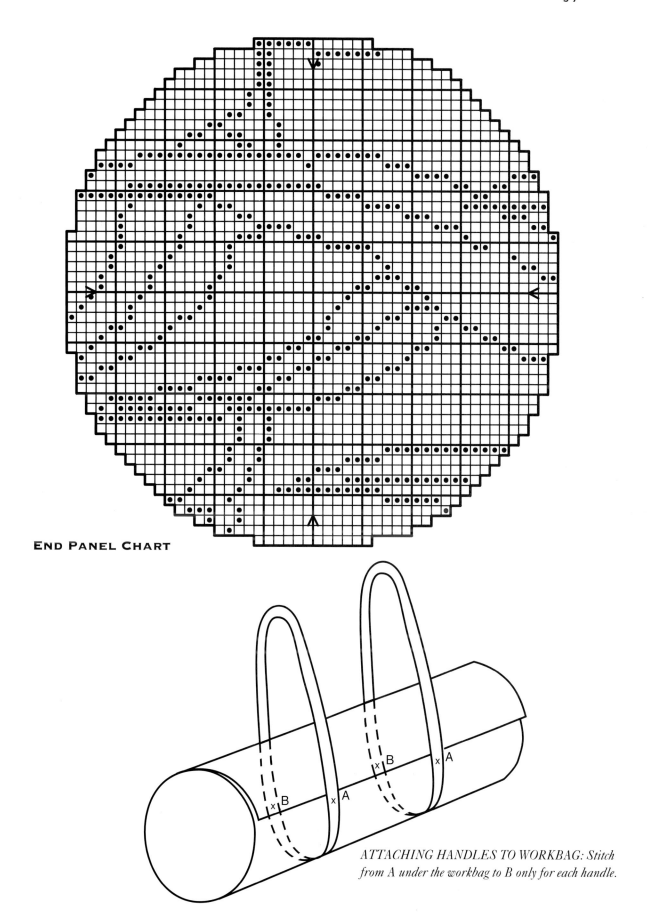

**END PANEL CHART**

*ATTACHING HANDLES TO WORKBAG: Stitch from A under the workbag to B only for each handle.*

*Flowers from Lisa Milasas*
*Jug from Linen and Lace of Balmain*

# Spring Blooms
## Sweet Pea glasses case

*Materials*
DMC Medici Wool (Art. 475) in the
following colours and skein quantities:

| | | | |
|---|---|---|---|
| 8101 | 1 | 8397 | 1 |
| 8118 | 2 | 8405 | 1 |
| 8151 | 1 | 8412 | 1 |
| 8211 | 1 | 8426 | 1 |
| 8224 | 1 | 8816 | 1 |
| 8329 | 5 | 8818 | 3 |
| 8331 | 1 | 8896 | 1 |
| 8332 | 1 | ecru | 1 |

DMC Stranded Cotton (Art. 117), 1 skein
each 223, 224 and 931
Zweigart Tapestry Canvas (Art. 604–70),
34 x 34 cm
Tapestry needle, size 24
Embroidery scissors
Roller tapestry frame
20 cm medium-weight cotton fabric, ecru
Machine cotton to match
Polyester blending machine thread, clear
Straw needle, size 4

Fold the canvas in half to find the centre
and tack a line down the centre fold. The
Sweet Pea design will be worked twice —
once into each half of the tapestry canvas.
Mount the canvas onto a roller frame.

Embroider the Sweet Pea design into the
centre of each half of the tapestry canvas
using Continental Stitch.
When the Continental Stitch part of the
design is complete, work the eyes with a
French Knot using one strand of 931.
Finally work the Back Stitch over single
rows of Continental Stitches as shown on
the chart.
Follow the finishing instructions given for
the Flannel Flower glasses case on pages
29–31.
Make the twisted cord by cutting four 2 m
lengths of both 8224 and 8818. Keep the
two colours separate. Keeping the threads
parallel, fold one colour in half and tie the
cut ends together in one knot. Keeping the
other coloured threads parallel, pass one
end through the folded end of the first
coloured thread, and tie the ends of the
second coloured thread together in one
knot. With these two looped-together
lengths of thread, make a twisted cord in
the same manner described on page 31 for
the Flannel Flower glasses case.
Attach the cord to the glasses case in the
same manner described on page 31.

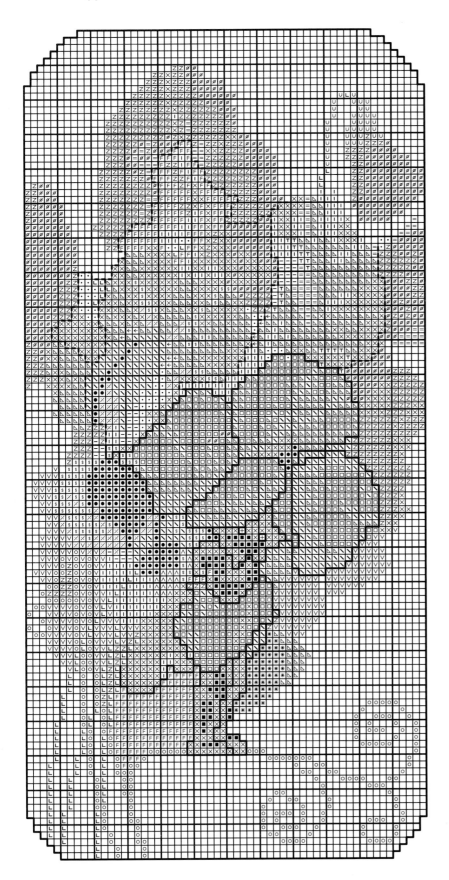

**KEY**

**MIXTURES:**

| | |
|---|---|
| Ⓢ | 8332+8816 |
| N | 8151+8818 |
| ⊡ | 8329+8818 |
| F | 8818+8118 |
| ⊟ | 8211+8118 |
| ⊠ | 8329+8118 |
| · | 8405+8118 |
| ✳ | 8331+8118 |
| ▪ | 8329+8118 |
| △ | 8332+8896 |

**PLAIN COLOURS:**

| | | |
|---|---|---|
| ⊞ | | ecru |
| T | 8397 | palest lilic |
| ← | 8896 | medium lilic |
| ⊟ | 8331 | pale greyish mauve |
| ⊠ | 8332 | jacaranda |
| ⊻ | 8211 | palest grey mauve |
| ⊠ | 8118 | palest greyish pink |
| ⊠ | 8818 | palest pink |
| I | 8151 | pale pink |
| N | 8816 | medium pink |
| ⊙ | 8101 | darkest pink |
| ⊙ | 8412 | dark yellow green |
| L | 8405 | light yellow green |
| ⊍ | 8426 | pale grey green |
| L | 223 | dark dusty pink (Art. 117) for back stitch – use 1 strand |
| L | 224 | mid dusty pink (Art. 117) for back stitch – use 1 strand |

# *Delphinium tiebacks*

## *Materials*

DMC Tapestry Wool (Art. 486) in the
following colours and skein quantities:

| | | | |
|------|---|------|---|
| 7120 | 2 | 7284 | 2 |
| 7121 | 1 | 7500 | 1 |
| 7213 | 1 | 7523 | 2 |
| 7230 | 1 | 7587 | 1 |
| 7232 | 1 | 7708 | 1 |
| 7241 | 4 | 7709 | 2 |
| 7255 | 1 | 7715 | 1 |
| 7260 | 1 | | |

DMC Tapestry Wool (Art. 487), 3 hanks
ecru
Zweigart Tapestry Canvas (Art. 604–48),
two pieces each 45 x 45 cm
Tapestry needle, size 22
Embroidery scissors
Roller tapestry frame
1 m medium-weight cotton fabric, ecru
Machine cotton to match
1 m woven interfacing (not iron-on)

2.3 m cotton piping cord
Polyester blending machine thread, clear
Straw needle, size 4

Use the matching points provided to join
Chart 2 to Chart 1 and Chart 3 to Chart 2.
You may prefer to photocopy the charts
and tape them together before starting the
needlepoint.
Mount one piece of tapestry canvas onto
the roller frame.
Measure 5 cm in and 5 cm down from the
top left hand corner of the canvas and start
the needlepoint at the top stitch on Chart 1.
The design should be worked in
Continental Stitch and the background
may be worked in either Continental
Stitch or Basketweave Stitch.
When the needlepoint is complete,
remove it from the frame and mount the
other piece of canvas.

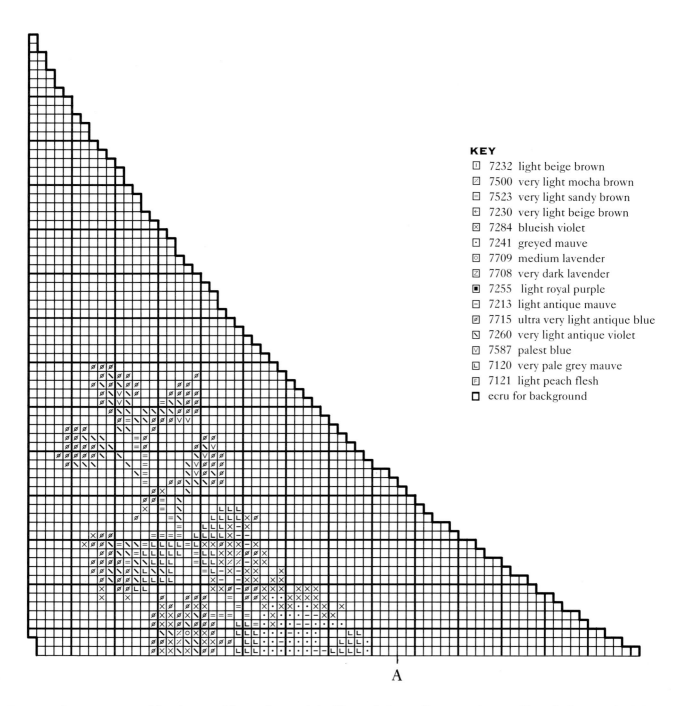

KEY
⊡ 7232 light beige brown
⊠ 7500 very light mocha brown
⊟ 7523 very light sandy brown
⊡ 7230 very light beige brown
⊠ 7284 blueish violet
⊡ 7241 greyed mauve
◎ 7709 medium lavender
⊠ 7708 very dark lavender
◾ 7255 light royal purple
⊟ 7213 light antique mauve
⊠ 7715 ultra very light antique blue
⊠ 7260 very light antique violet
⊻ 7587 palest blue
⊡ 7120 very pale grey mauve
⊟ 7121 light peach flesh
☐ ecru for background

A

**CHART 1**

Use the matching points to join Charts 4, 5 and 6 as described above.

Measure 5 cm in and 5 cm down from the top right hand corner of the canvas and start the needlepoint at the top of the stitching on Chart 4.

Remove the second canvas from the frame and block both pieces.

Make a tracing of the Tieback Pattern on pages 44 and 45.

Cut two pieces of interfacing on the fold as indicated. Cut a further four pieces of interfacing the exact size of the Tieback Pattern.

Pin a piece of interfacing to the back of each needlepoint tieback section. Slip stitch the interfacing to the back of the needlepoint.

Cut two full lining pieces of ecru fabric using the Tieback Pattern, placing the fold

**CHART 2**

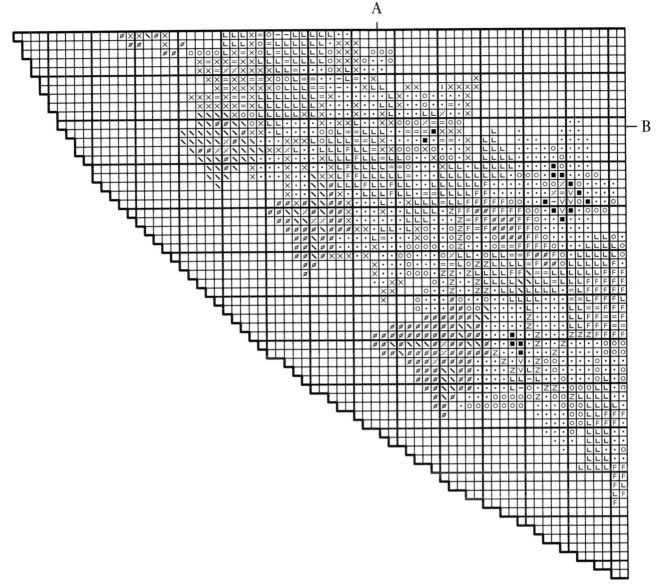

end on the fold of the fabric and adding 1.5 cm seam allowance to all other edges. Cut two half lining pieces of ecru fabric using the Tieback Pattern and adding 1.5 cm seam allowance to all edges.

Interface each lining section with a matching piece of interfacing, taking care to interface the single lining sections in opposite directions. One tieback is for the left curtain and the other is for the right curtain, so they will be mirror images of each other.

Pin one interfaced needlepoint section to its appropriate interfaced single lining section along the straight seam (this is the one indicated by "fold" on the Tieback

Pattern) with right sides together. (Note: the interfaced sides of both sections will be outermost.) Stitch the sections together along this seam one needlepoint row in from the edge of the needlepoint. Repeat for the other tieback, ensuring that it is a mirror image of the first one. Fold both seam allowances behind the single lining section, and tack the seam allowances back to hold them in position.

From the remaining fabric, cut enough bias strips to make 2.3 m of bias. Join the strips, press seam allowances open and make into piping, following the instructions on pages 15 and 20.

CHART 3

B

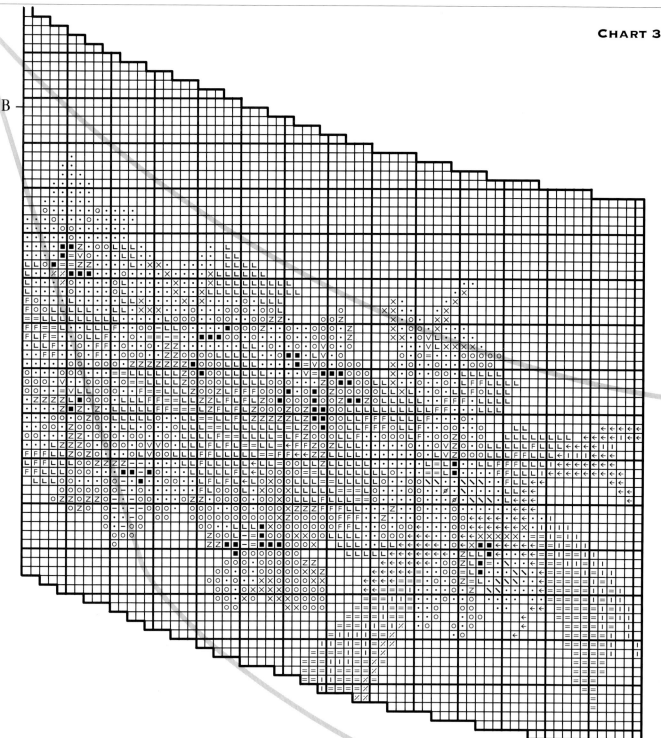

Pin the piping to the right side of the needlepoint, approximately one row in from the edge of the needlepoint starting at the lower edge of the tieback, making sure that the piping takes a smooth curve around the needlepoint and a matching curve around the lining piece. Clip the seam allowance on the piping so that it will lie smoothly. The piping must be pivoted at the sharp top corners of the tiebacks, so the seam allowance on the piping will need to be clipped several times. Unpick as much stitching in the piping as necessary and join the ends of the bias to fit the needlepoint. Place the piping cord back into the bias and restitch it into

**CHART 4**

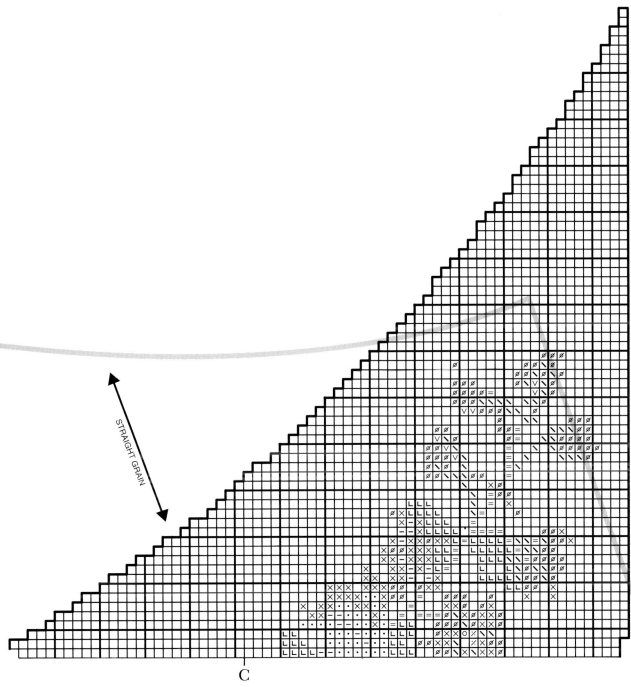

STRAIGHT GRAIN

C

FOLDLINE FOR LININGS ONLY

position, overlapping the cord in the piping channel and machining over the overlapped cord (see pages 15 and 20). Stitch the piping into position around the tiebacks, using the zipper foot on the sewing machine.

Turn back the seam allowances towards the wrong sides of the tiebacks and tack.

Stitch between every third or fourth needlepoint stitch with a doubled length of the clear polyester blending thread in the straw needle, stitching around the needlepoint sections of the tiebacks only. Cut four pieces of ecru fabric each 10 x 2 cm wide for loops. Fold one strip of fabric into half lengthwise and press (see figure i

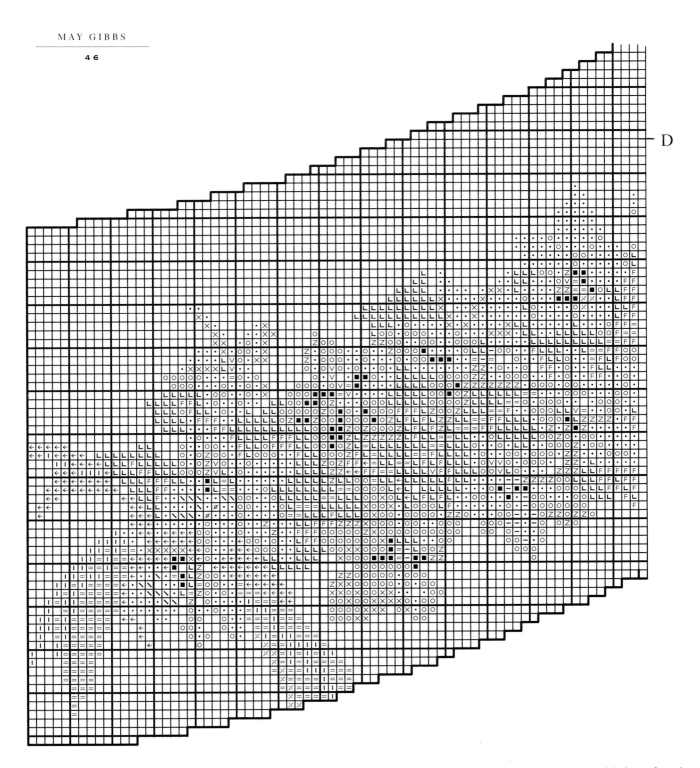

D

**CHART 5**

on page 47). Turn in each long raw edge again to the centre fold line and press. Fold the strip along the first fold line and slip stitch the second fold lines together by hand (or machine if preferred). Repeat for the other three small strips of fabric.

Each of these strips is a loop to be attached to the points of the tiebacks. Attach each loop as shown in figure ii.

Pin an interfaced full lining piece to the back of each piped section with interfaced sides together. Turn in the seam allowances and clip the curves as necessary so that each lining section fits neatly inside the piping. Slip stitch the linings into position.

Each Delphinium tieback will wrap around a curtain and the loops at each point will slip over a hook fastened to the wall behind the edge of the curtain.

**CHART 6**

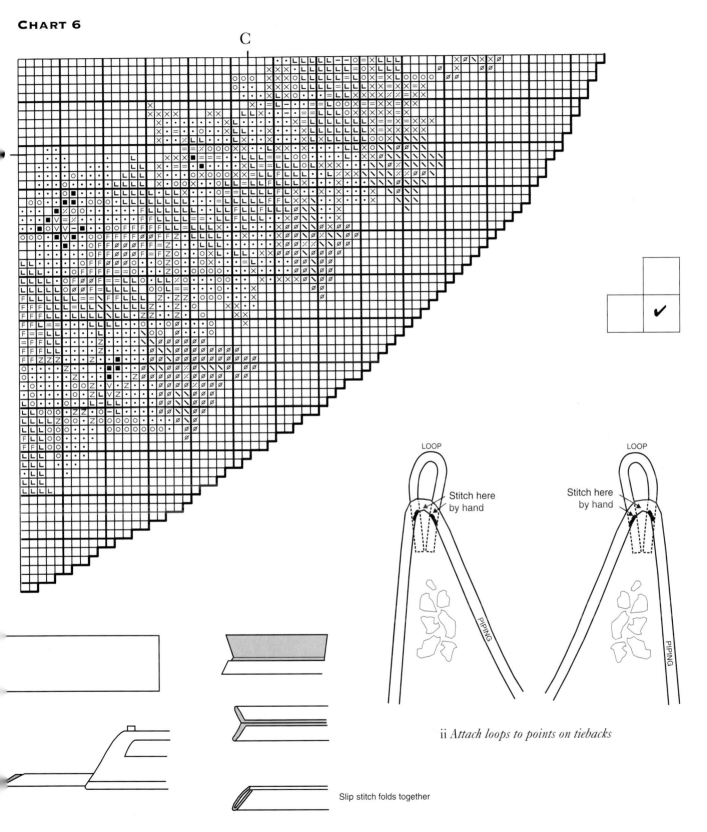

i *Make fabric loops for tiebacks*

Slip stitch folds together

LOOP

Stitch here by hand

PIPING

LOOP

Stitch here by hand

PIPING

ii *Attach loops to points on tiebacks*

*Curtain fabric from Wardlaw*
*Basket from Linen and Lace of Balmain*
*Framing by Essex Framing Company*

LITTLE RAGGED
BLOSSOM

*And more about*
*Snugglepot and Cuddlepie*

# Bushland

## Little Ragged Blossom box

*Materials*

DMC Tapestry Wool (Art. 486) in the following colours and skein quantities:

| | | | |
|------|---|------|---|
| 7121 | 1 | 7466 | 2 |
| 7191 | 1 | 7470 | 2 |
| 7304 | 1 | 7544 | 1 |
| 7351 | 1 | 7702 | 1 |
| 7361 | 1 | 7760 | 1 |
| 7372 | 1 | 7840 | 2 |
| 7384 | 1 | 7853 | 1 |
| 7408 | 1 | 7938 | 2 |
| 7448 | 2 | | |

DMC Stranded Cotton (Art. 117), 1 skein 3773

Zweigart Tapestry Canvas (Art. 604–48), 30 x 30 cm

Tapestry needle, size 22

Embroidery scissors

Roller tapestry frame

22 cm diameter round wooden box

FolkArt paints, 1 bottle each of the following colours:

    745 Huckleberry

    750 Spice Pink

    757 Brownie

    935 Raspberry Wine

FolkArt Extender

FolkArt Thickener

2.5 cm sponge brush

Marbling sponge

FolkArt Hi-Shine Aerosol Glaze

Paper plate

25 x 25 cm heavy cardboard or strawboard

Strong thread or wool for lacing

Craft glue

Find the centre of each side of the canvas and mount it onto the roller frame.

The centre of the canvas corresponds to the centre of the chart. Start the needlepoint at the centre. Work the needlepoint using Continental Stitch.

When the needlepoint is complete, work the Back Stitch details with one strand of 3773. Work the French Knots with one full thickness of 7470.

Remove the canvas from the frame and block it.

Cut out a circle of cardboard with the diameter of the bottom of the box. Cut out the needlepoint leaving a 2 cm seam allowance of unworked canvas all around it. Place the cardboard on the wrong side of the needlepoint and thread the tapestry needle with a long length of strong thread or wool. Lace the canvas around the cardboard, easing the fullness of canvas evenly around the circle.

Base coat the inside and outside of the box with two coats of Brownie using the sponge brush.

On the paper plate, squeeze out a 9 cm circle of Huckleberry, Spice Pink and Raspberry Wine (not a puddle — just squeeze the bottle and squirt out a roughly circular outline). Squeeze out a puddle of Extender and Thickener into the paint colours and mix them only once in a figure-8 pattern with your finger.

Pick out pieces of the marbling sponge to give it an irregular surface. Wet the sponge

with water and squeeze it out well. Dab
the picked-out side of the sponge into the
paint once or twice to pick up patches of
colour. Dab the sponge onto the outside of
the box and the outside rim of the box lid.
Use a gentle press-down-and-lift movement
— don't move the sponge sideways and try

not to overlap the colour dabs too much.
Allow the marbling to dry thoroughly before
applying several coats of Hi-Shine Glaze to
the inside and outside of the box and its
lid, following the instructions on the can.
Glue the laced needlepoint onto the top of
the lid of the box.

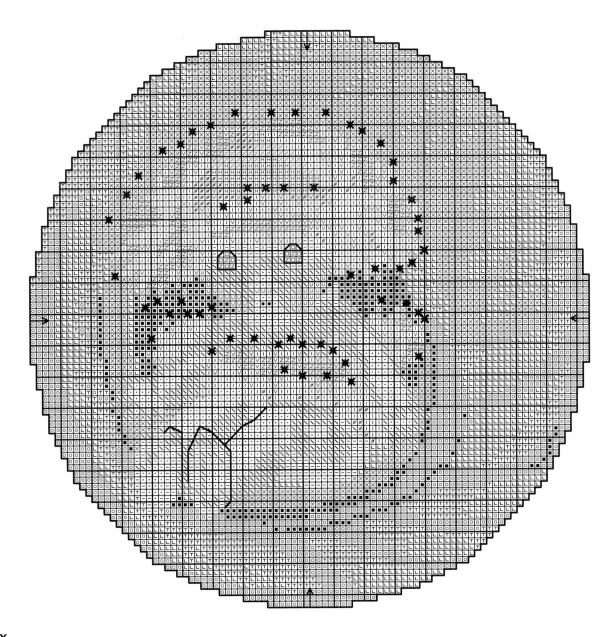

## KEY

| | | | | | |
|---|---|---|---|---|---|
| ▣ | 7372 ultra very dark wine red | ⊟ | 7853 peach flesh | ☑ | 7470 ultra very light avocado green |
| ⊙ | 7938 dark twill brown | ⊍ | 7760 salmon | ⊠ | 7351 very light avocado green |
| ⊤ | 7448 very dark rose brown | ⊞ | 7304 medium baby blue | ⊡ | 7361 very light lime green |
| ⊥ | 7840 medium negro flesh | ⊠ | 7702 medium blue green | ✳ | 7470 ultra very light avocado green for |
| ☒ | 7466 medium forest brown | ⊞ | 7384 medium yellow green | | french knots – use full thickness of wool |
| ⊡ | 7191 very light peach flesh | ⊠ | 7408 dark bush green | ⌐ | 3773 dark skin pink (Art. 117) for |
| ⊠ | 7121 light peach flesh | ▣ | 7544 christmas red | | outlines – use 1 strand |

# Rambling Flowers picture

## Materials

DMC Tapestry Wool (Art. 486) in the following colours and skein quantities:

| | | | |
|---|---|---|---|
| 7108 | 1 | 7423 | 1 |
| 7139 | 1 | 7446 | 1 |
| 7175 | 1 | 7457 | 1 |
| 7176 | 1 | 7493 | 1 |
| 7228 | 1 | 7515 | 1 |
| 7331 | 1 | 7703 | 1 |
| 7347 | 1 | 7739 | 1 |
| 7370 | 3 | 7870 | 1 |
| 7392 | 1 | 7922 | 1 |
| 7394 | 1 | ecru | 1 |

DMC Tapestry Wool (Art. 487), 6 hanks 7500
Zweigart Tapestry Canvas (Art. 604–48),
43 x 38 cm
Tapestry needle, size 22
Embroidery scissors
Roller tapestry frame

Find the centre of the canvas both vertically and horizontally and tack a centre line across the canvas at each centre mark. Mount the long edges of the canvas onto the roller frame.

Align the rectangular shape of the chart with the rectangular shape of the canvas. Start the needlepoint at the centre of the design and work the floral section with Continental Stitch. Work the background with Basketweave Stitch.

Remove the needlepoint from the frame and block it.

Take the needlepoint to a framer for professional mounting and finishing. The outline on this page will show the framer how to cut out the shaped mount shown in this photograph. Please note the outline is 50% of actual size.

## KEY

| | | | | | | |
|---|---|---|---|---|---|---|
| ⊡ | ecru | ⊡ | 7457 orange mustard | ▲ | 7922 bright mahogany |
| ⊞ | 7331 light grey green | ▣ | 7515 black brown | ⊟ | 7739 light brownie |
| ⊞ | 7870 very light fern green | ⑤ | 7108 red | ⊡ | 7493 light sand |
| ⊡ | 7392 light fern green | ⊤ | 7139 dark cherry | ☒ | 7423 sand |
| ⊻ | 7703 light blue green | ◩ | 7228 wine red | ☐ | 7500 very light mocha brown |
| ☒ | 7370 light tartan green | ⊡ | 7175 light orange | | for background |
| ◉ | 7347 ultra very dark parrot green | ⊟ | 7176 mid orange | | |
| ◨ | 7394 fern green | ⊻ | 7446 dark orange | | |

CHART 1

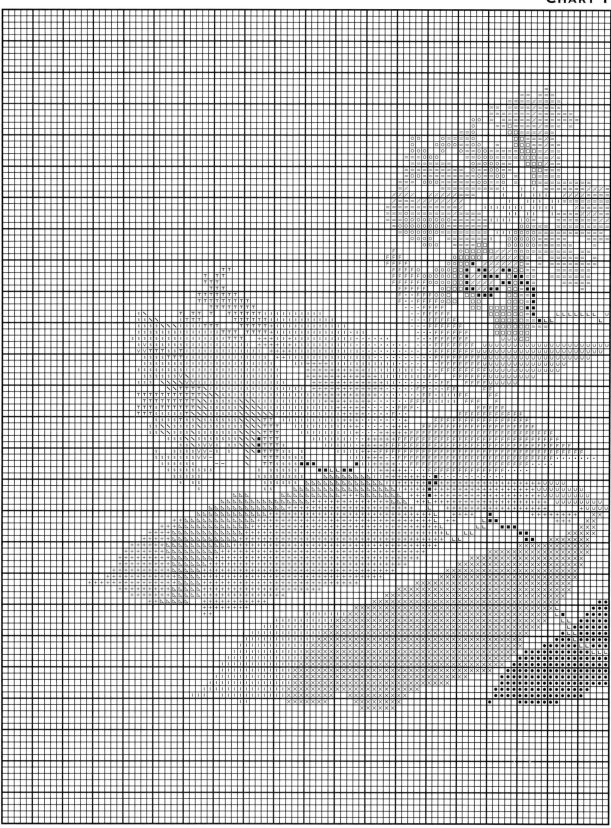

# CHART 2

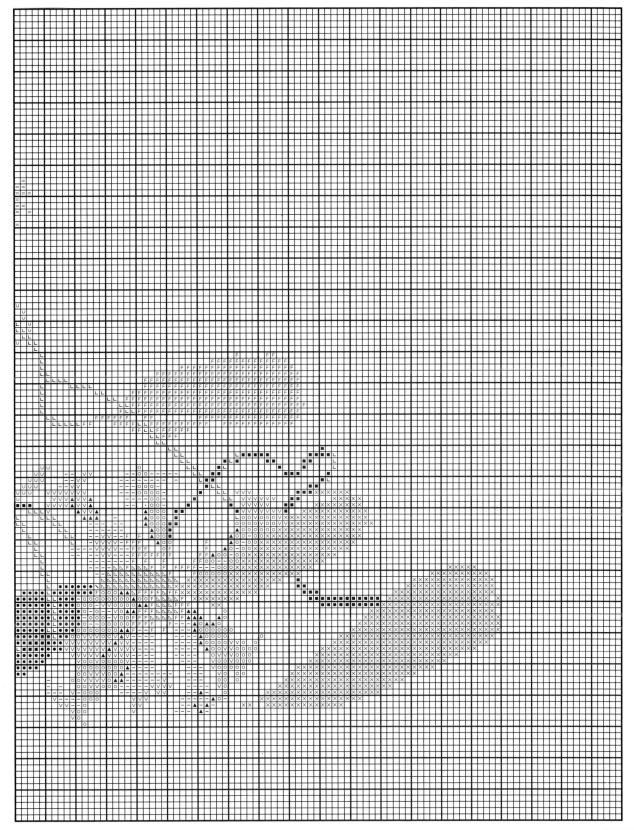

# *Fancy that!*

## *Blue & white border cushion*

*Materials*

DMC Tapestry Wool (Art. 487), 5 hanks 7300

DMC Pearl 3 Cotton (Art. 115) in the following colours and skein quantities:

| | |
|---|---|
| 322 | 4 |
| 336 | 1 |
| 930 | 10 |

Zweigart Tapestry Canvas (Art. 604–48), 34 x 34 cm

Tapestry needle, size 22

Embroidery scissors

Roller tapestry frame

40 cm medium-weight cotton fabric to match 322

Machine cotton to match

35 x 35 cm cushion insert

Straw needle, size 4

Two 10 x 10 cm squares of cardboard

Mount the canvas onto the roller frame. Measure 5 cm in and 5 cm down from the top left hand corner of the canvas. This point corresponds with the top left hand corner of the chart. Count in the appropriate number of stitches to the beginning of the blue pattern and start the needlepoint here. Work the blues in Continental Stitch and the background in Basketweave Stitch, leaving an unstitched square in the centre of the canvas. When the needlepoint is complete, remove it from the frame and block it.

Cut a piece of blue cotton fabric 40 x 40 cm and another piece 22 x 22 cm and press them.

Pin the smaller piece of fabric onto the unworked square in the middle of the canvas, with the wrong side of the fabric facing the right side of the canvas. Turn under the raw edges of the fabric in position so that the folded edge of the fabric covers the innermost row of needlepoint. Slip stitch the fabric to the canvas with small invisible stitches, using the blue machine thread in the straw needle.

Pin together the larger square of blue fabric and the needlepoint with right sides facing. Machine stitch the two layers together, one row in from the edge of the needlepoint, leaving an unstitched gap of approximately 26 cm in the centre of one side.

Trim seam allowances to 1.5 cm. Zigzag the raw edges, taking care to zigzag each side of the gap separately. Turn the cushion right sides out.

Push the cushion insert into the cushion and slip stitch the gap closed except for the last 2 cm; don't end off the thread.

**TWISTED CORD**

Cut twelve 4.5 m lengths from the extra skeins of 930. Make a twisted cord using these threads, following the instructions on page 31.

Push the folded end of the twisted cord into the gap in the bottom of the cushion

**KEY**

- ⊠ 336 dark blue
- ⊡ 930 greyed blue
- ⊡ 322 mid blue
- ☐ 7300 very light grey for background

and stitch the cord all around the edge of the cushion; again, don't end off the thread. Tie a knot in the other end of the cord about 2 cm beyond where it will be pushed into the gap in the bottom of the cushion. Cut off any excess cord beyond the knot and push the knot inside the cushion. Rethread the needle with the slip stitching thread and finish closing the lower edge of the cushion, passing the needle through both ends of the cord while doing so.

Rethread the needle with the thread used for attaching the cord and complete stitching the cord to the cushion.

**TASSELS**

Each tassel will need one skein of 930. Open out a skein and cut off two lengths each 40 cm long. Place the two squares of cardboard on top of each other and pass one 40 cm length between the two squares of cardboard. Wind the thread around the two pieces of cardboard 65 times, starting and ending at the same side of the cardboard. Take the ends of the thread which are between the cardboard squares and tie together securely and very close to the wound thread. Slide the cardboard out from between the threads.

Smooth down the threads of the tassel until they lie neatly. Wrap the other 40 cm length of thread around the tassel 1.5 cm below the top. Tie the ends of the wrapping thread together tightly and thread them onto a needle one at a time; pass the needle behind the wrapping and pull it out below in the skirt of the tassel. Pull these two threads tightly to pull the knot down behind the wrapping. Cut the loops of the tassel and trim its skirt evenly. Make three other tassels in the same manner. It is a good idea to trim the tassels together to make sure they are the same length.

Tie a tassel to the cord at each corner of the cushion. Make sure that it is tied on tightly and as close to the cord as possible. Thread the tying threads into a needle and bury the ends in the cushion.

# Pretty in Pinks
## Baby Faces
## doorstop

### Materials

DMC Tapestry Wool (Art. 486) in the following colours and skein quantities:

| | | | |
|------|---|------|---|
| 7120 | 2 | 7494 | 1 |
| 7121 | 1 | 7511 | 1 |
| 7122 | 2 | 7759 | 2 |
| 7191 | 1 | 7760 | 1 |
| 7200 | 2 | 7761 | 2 |
| 7213 | 1 | 7800 | 1 |
| 7260 | 1 | 7853 | 1 |
| 7398 | 1 | 7870 | 1 |
| 7426 | 1 | ecru | 1 |
| 7492 | 3 | | |

DMC Stranded Cotton (Art. 117), 1 skein 3772
Zweigart Tapestry Canvas (Art. 604–48), 33 x 23 cm
Tapestry needle, size 22
Embroidery scissors
Roller tapestry frame
30 cm medium-weight cotton fabric, apricot pink
Machine cotton to match
Polyester wadding
Brick or piece of heavy wood to fit the needlepoint (If using a brick, it must be totally dry. It may need baking in the oven to dry it out thoroughly)
Strong thread or wool for lacing
Straw needle, size 3 or 4

Mount the long sides of the canvas onto the frame.

Measure 5 cm in and 5 cm down from the top right hand corner of the canvas. This point corresponds with the top right hand stitch on the chart. Start the needlepoint here. Work the design using Continental Stitch.

When the needlepoint is complete, use two strands of 3772 to work the eyelashes. Each eyelash is one long stitch.

Remove the canvas from the frame and block it.

Cut two pieces of wadding for each of the six sides of the doorstop and oversew them together by hand to form a box shape. Before the last side is sewn into position, fit the wood or brick into the inside.

From the cotton fabric, cut two pieces 26 x 13 cm, two pieces 16 x 13 cm and one piece 26 x 16 cm.(These measurements include a 2cm seam allowance on all sides.) Matching the centres on each side of the canvas to the centre of each side of the pieces of fabric, sew a long piece of fabric (26 x 13 cm) to each long side of the needlepoint, and a short piece (16 x 13 cm) to each short side of the needlepoint. Carefully place the 13 cm lengths of these fabric together so that they are even, and sew up the sides of the doorstop.

Trim the seam allowances. Turn the doorstop right side out and fit over the padded wooden form or brick.

Lace the seam allowances along the bottom of the doorstop to and fro, using the strong thread or wool, so that the canvas is held snugly around the doorstop. Cover the laced bottom of the doorstop with the larger piece of fabric, turn under the raw edges and slip stitch into place using a doubled length of machine thread in the straw needle.

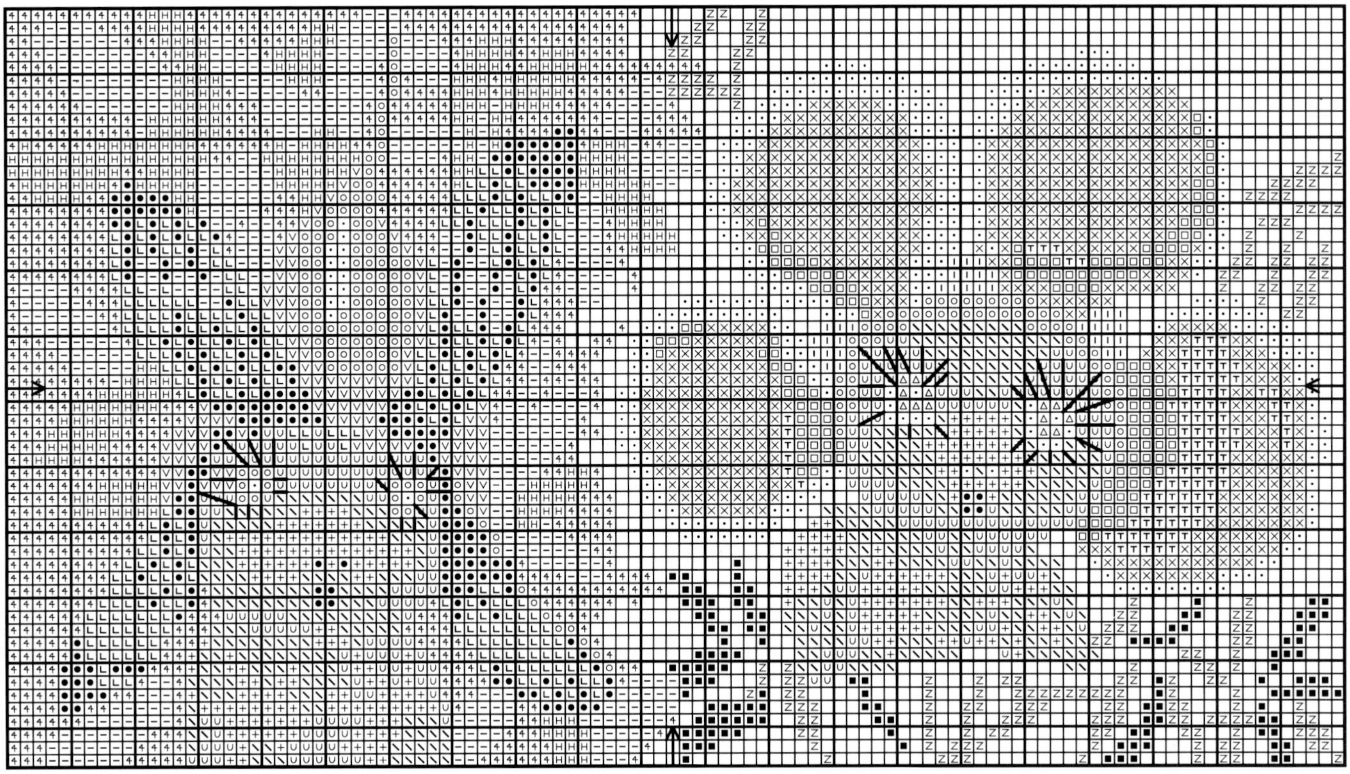

**KEY**

- ● 7759 medium salmon
- L 7760 salmon
- – 7761 light salmon
- H 7122 very light salmon pink
- O 7511 light drab brown
- V 7494 golden brown
- · ecru
- ■ 7398 very dark pine green
- I 7426 medium eucalyptus green
- Z 7870 very light fern green
- ◻ 7213 light antique mauve
- X 7200 ultra very light dusty rose
- T 7260 very light antique violet
- △ 7800 very light baby blue
- + 7191 very light peach flesh
- \ 7121 light peach flesh
- U 7853 peach flesh
- 4 7492 very light drab brown
- ☐ 7120 very pale grey mauve
- ┐ 3772 medium skin pink (Art. 117) for eyelashes – use 2 strands

# Riding Home the Dragons cushion

## Materials

DMC Tapestry Wool (Art. 486) in the following colours and skein quantities:

| | | | |
|---|---|---|---|
| 7107 | 1 | 7413 | 1 |
| 7121 | 1 | 7453 | 2 |
| 7144 | 1 | 7421 | 1 |
| 7170 | 1 | 7520 | 1 |
| 7174 | 1 | 7579 | 1 |
| 7193 | 2 | 7587 | 4 |
| 7194 | 2 | 7709 | 1 |
| 7213 | 2 | 7739 | 1 |
| 7241 | 6 | 7746 | 8 |
| 7255 | 1 | 7802 | 1 |
| 7321 | 2 | 7928 | 5 |
| 7369 | 1 | ecru | 6 |
| 7370 | 1 | black | 1 |
| 7400 | 1 | | |

DMC Stranded Cotton (Art. 117), 1 skein
839
Zweigart Tapestry Canvas (Art. 604–6048),
53 x 40 cm
Tapestry needle, size 22
Embroidery scissors
Roller tapestry frame
42 x 30 cm cushion insert
50 cm medium-weight cotton fabric,
dusty pink
Machine cotton to match
1.6 m cotton piping cord

Mount the long sides of the canvas onto the roller frame.

Measure 5 cm in and 5 cm down from the top left hand side of the canvas. This point corresponds with the top left hand stitch on Chart 1. Start the needlepoint here. Work the needlepoint in Continental Stitch.

When the needlepoint is complete, work the Back Stitches around the eye with two strands of 839.

Remove the canvas from the frame and block it.

From the cotton fabric cut a rectangle of backing fabric 50 x 35 cm and 1.6 m bias for the piping. Make the bias into piping (see instructions on pages 15 and 20).

Make up the piped cushion following the instructions given on pages 15 and 20.

## CHART 1

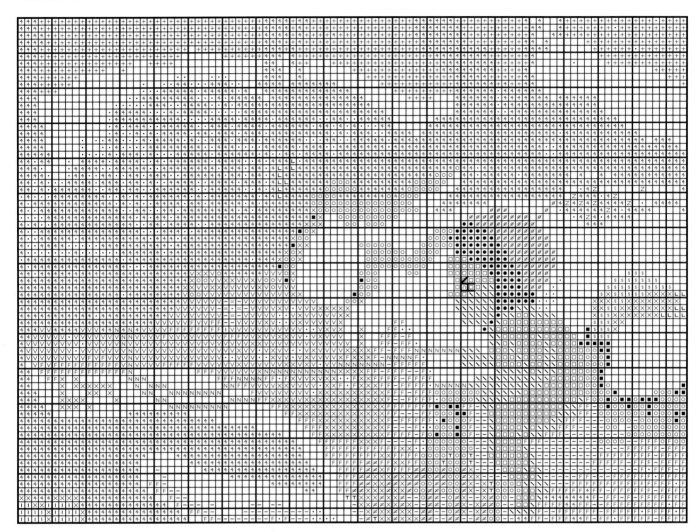

## KEY

| | | | | | | |
|---|---|---|---|---|---|---|
| ⊡ | 7255 light royal purple | ⊟ | black | ☑ | 7587 palest blue |
| ⊡ | 7709 medium lavender | ⮡ | 7213 light antique mauve | ☑ | 7400 ultra very light bush green |
| ⊞ | 7453 ultra very light brownie | ④ | 7241 greyed mauve | ⊠ | 7321 ultra very light greenish grey |
| ⊻ | 7739 light brownie | ⊡ | 7370 light tartan green | ⊠ | 7520 medium mocha brown |
| ⊟ | 7421 very light brown | ⊠ | 7369 very light tartan green | ⊞ | 7413 medium drab brown |
| ⊡ | ecru | ⊡ | 7170 pinkish white | ❑ | 7746 off white |
| ■ | 7107 bright red | ⊠ | 7121 light peach flesh | ⌐ | 839 pale brown (Art. 117) for eye and |
| ⊡ | 7194 light shell pink | ⌂ | 7802 baby blue | | eyelashes – use 1 strand |
| ⊠ | 7193 very light shell pink | ⊡ | 7202 light dusty rose | | |
| ⊡ | 7144 light camel | ⊡ | 7579 very light golden brown | | |
| ⊡ | 7174 light forest brown | ⊞ | 7928 ultra very light grey green | | |

# CHART 2

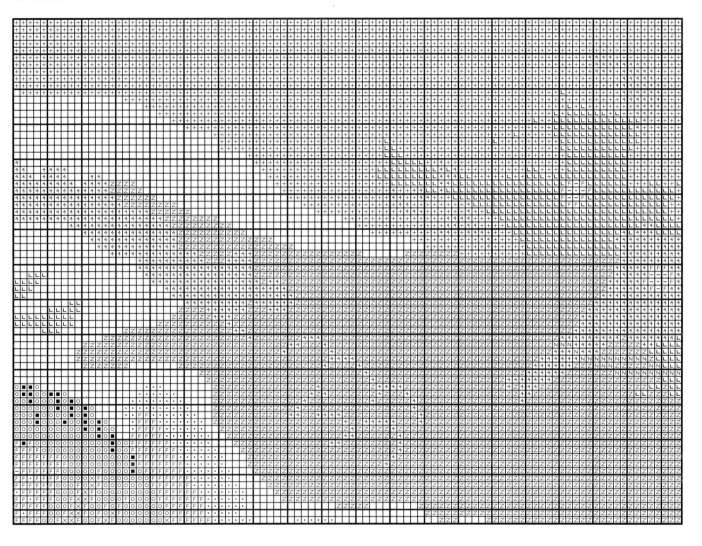

## CHART 3

## CHART 4

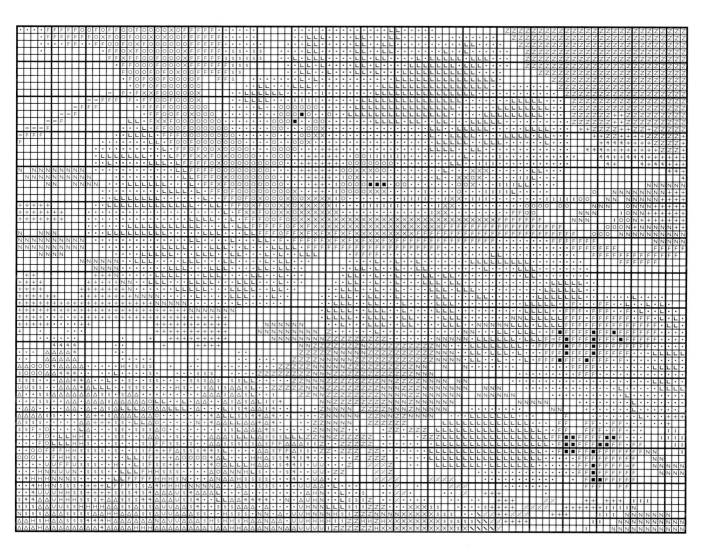

# Midnight May
## Possum cushion

*Materials*

DMC Tapestry Wool (Art. 486) in the
following colours and skein quantities:
7191          10
7336          8
Zweigart Tapestry Canvas (Art. 604–48),
32 x 32 cm
Tapestry needle, size 22
Embroidery scissors
Roller tapestry frame
60 cm cotton velveteen, navy blue
Machine cotton to match
35 x 35 cm cushion insert
Set square

Mount the canvas onto the roller frame.
Find the centre of the canvas and the centre
of the chart and start the needlepoint here.
Work the outlines in Continental Stitch
and the background in Basketweave Stitch.
When the needlepoint is complete, remove
the canvas from the frame and block it.
Cut the following pieces of fabric from the
velveteen: one piece 40 x 40 cm, two strips
40 x 12 cm across the velveteen and two
strips 40 x 12 cm down the velveteen.
NOTE: The strips are cut in each
specified direction on the velveteen
because of its nap. When the strips are
sewn on around the needlepoint, ensure
that the nap of the velveteen is always in
the same direction, otherwise the fabric
will appear to be different colours.
Press all pieces of velveteen.

Sew a strip of velveteen fabric onto each
side of the needlepoint, matching the
centre on the long side of each strip to the
centre on a side of the needlepoint. A 1.5
cm seam allowance has been included in
the measurements given. On each side,
stop the stitching precisely at the edge of
the needlepoint — don't run on with the
stitching.
Put the ends of each strip squarely
together with right sides facing. Use the
set square to pin each corner into a mitre.
Open out each seam before stitching it to
check that the mitre is neat; adjust as
necessary. Stitch each mitred corner.
Open out the frame of the cushion. Trim
the seam allowances on the mitre and
around the canvas.  Press open the seam
allowances on the mitred corners.
Measure 7.5 cm outside the seam where
the canvas joins the frame and tack a line
around the cushion which is consistently
7.5 cm outside the needlepoint. This is the
stitching line for the outside of the cushion.
Put the framed needlepoint and the square
of backing fabric together with right sides
facing. Pin the two layers together.
Machine stitch around the cushion,
following the tacked line, leaving a 28 cm
unstitched gap along the bottom of the
cushion. Stitch around the corners in a
gentle curve so that the corners of the
cushion are not too pointed.
Trim seam allowances to 1.5 cm. Zigzag

**KEY**

⊡ 7336 navy blue
☐ 7191 very light peach flesh for background

around the raw edges, remembering to zigzag each side of the gap in the cushion. Turn the cushion right side out.
Push the cushion insert into the cushion and slip stitch the gap closed except for the last 2 cm; don't end off the slip stitching thread.

**TWISTED CORD**
Cut one 4.5 m length of 7191 and five 4.5 m lengths of 7336. Put the threads together and make a twisted cord following the instructions on page 31. Attach the cord, following the instructions on pages 55–57. When both ends of the cord are securely inside the cushion, finish with the slip stitching thread which was used to close the cushion.

# *Midnight cushion*

*Materials*

DMC Tapestry Wool (Art. 486) in the following colours and skein quantities:

| | | | |
|------|----|------|----|
| 7108 | 1 | 7519 | 8 |
| 7121 | 1 | 7521 | 2 |
| 7299 | 1 | 7533 | 1 |
| 7331 | 3 | 7622 | 5 |
| 7336 | 5 | 7802 | 1 |
| 7362 | 1 | 7853 | 1 |
| 7413 | 3 | 7870 | 2 |
| 7426 | 1 | 7905 | 1 |
| 7491 | 3 | 7925 | 17 |
| 7499 | 1 | | |

DMC Stranded Cotton (Art. 117), 1 skein each 3078, 3772 and 3773
Kreinik Metallic Thread Balger Cable 001P silver, 1 reel (use 3 thicknesses of the thread)
Zweigart Tapestry Canvas (Art. 604–48), 45 x 45 cm
Tapestry needle, size *22*
Embroidery scissors
Roller tapestry frame
40 cm cotton velveteen fabric, navy blue
Machine cotton to match
Machine cotton to match taupe 7622
35 x 35 cm cushion insert
Straw needle, size 4

Mount the canvas onto the roller frame. Measure 5 cm in and 5 cm down from the top right hand side of the canvas. This point corresponds with the top right stitch on Chart 2. Start work here using Basketweave Stitch. Count the rows carefully as you work until enough background has been worked to start the taupe and grey circle around the centre section of the design. Work the centre design in Continental Stitch.

When the needlepoint is complete, add the Back Stitch details and the French Knots. When the needlepoint is complete, remove the canvas from the frame and block it. Cut a piece of fabric 38 x 38 cm. Press it and make up the cushion following the instructions on pages 67–68.

**TWISTED CORD**

Cut three 4.5 m lengths of 7622 and five 4.5 m lengths of 7519. Put all the threads together and make a twisted cord according to the instructions on page 31. Attach the twisted cord to the cushion in the same way as described on pages 55–57.

# CHART 1

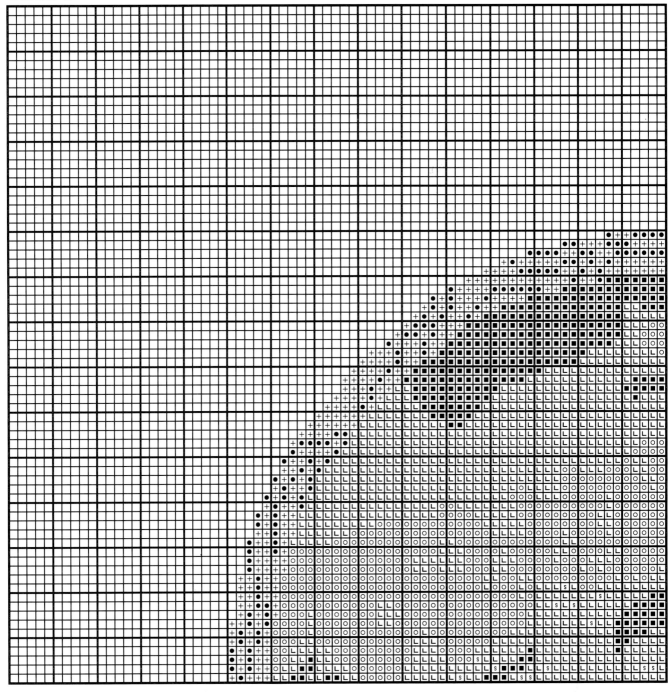

## KEY

◻ 7925 very dark peacock blue for
background
▣ 7299 very dark blue
L 7336 navy blue
◙ 7491 very light rose beige
s silver
▪ 7622 dark pewter grey
⊞ 7519 mocha brown
◪ 7499 very dark coffee brown

▫ 7870 very light fern green
T 7331 light grey green
▽ 7413 medium drab brown
⊞ 7521 grey mist
▨ 7533 very dark forest brown
◿ 7362 light lime green
⊍ 7426 medium eucalyptus green
▣ 7108 red
▶ 7802 baby blue
✕ 7121 light peach flesh

⊟ 7853 peach flesh
⊟ 7905 ultra very light golden yellow
— 3773 dark skin pink (Art. 117) for body
outlines and noses – use 2 strands
- 3772 darkest skin pink for eyelashes – use
2 strands
✳ 3078 yellow (Art. 117)
for french knots on
blossom and pupils –
use 2 strands

**CHART 2**

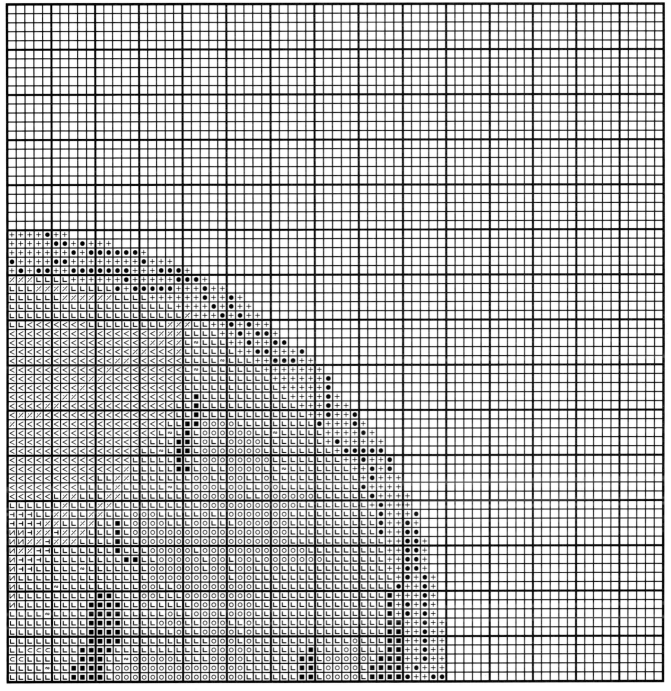

# CHART 3

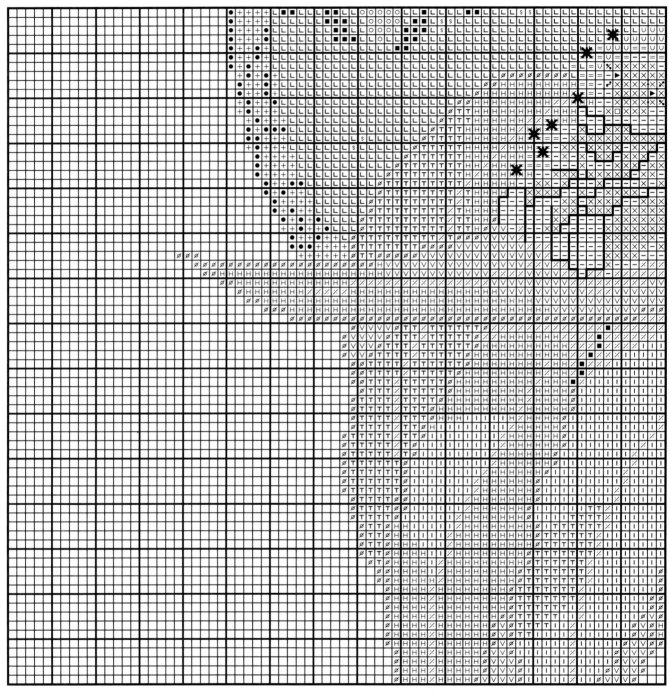

## CHART 4

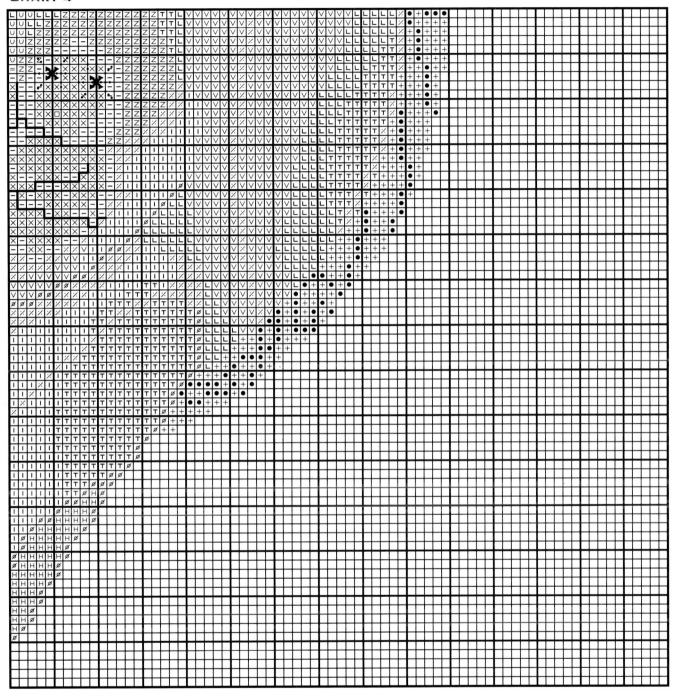

# Gumleaves
## Naughty Mantis cushion

*Materials*

DMC Tapestry Wool (Art. 486) in the following colours and skein quantities:

| | | | |
|------|---|-------|---|
| 7121 | 1 | 7500 | 1 |
| 7215 | 1 | 7504 | 1 |
| 7264 | 2 | 7582 | 1 |
| 7356 | 1 | 7802 | 1 |
| 7370 | 3 | 7928 | 1 |
| 7394 | 2 | ecru | 1 |
| 7491 | 9 | black | 1 |

DMC Stranded Cotton (Art. 117), 1 skein each 310, 3042 and 3772
Zweigart Tapestry Canvas (Art. 604–48), 35 x 35 cm
Tapestry needle, size 22
Embroidery scissors
Roller tapestry frame
60 cm medium-weight cotton fabric, grey green
Machine cotton to match
1.6 m cotton piping cord
35 x 35 cm cushion insert

Find the centre of the canvas horizontally and vertically and tack centre lines. Mount the canvas onto the roller frame. Find the centre of the chart. These two centres correspond. Start the needlepoint here. Work the design in Continental Stitch and the background in Basketweave Stitch. When the needlepoint is complete, work the Back Stitch details using the number of strands indicated in the key. Remove the canvas from the frame and block it.

Cut the following pieces from the fabric: one piece 40 x 40 cm, four strips 11 x 40 cm and 1.8 m bias (see pages 15 and 20 for instructions on cutting bias).

Make up the framed cushion following the instructions on pages 67–68. This cushion is piped, so once the frame has been attached to the needlepoint, the corners mitred and the stitching line tacked 7 cm outside the seam joining the frame to the needlepoint, add the piping. (See instructions on pages 15 and 20).

Apply the backing to the cushion with right sides together, pin the layers together. Stitch closely around the outside of the piping, leaving a 28 cm gap in the bottom of the cushion. Trim seam allowances and zigzag raw edges, taking care to zigzag each side of the opening in the cushion. Turn the cushion right side out. Push the insert into the cushion and slip stitch the opening closed.

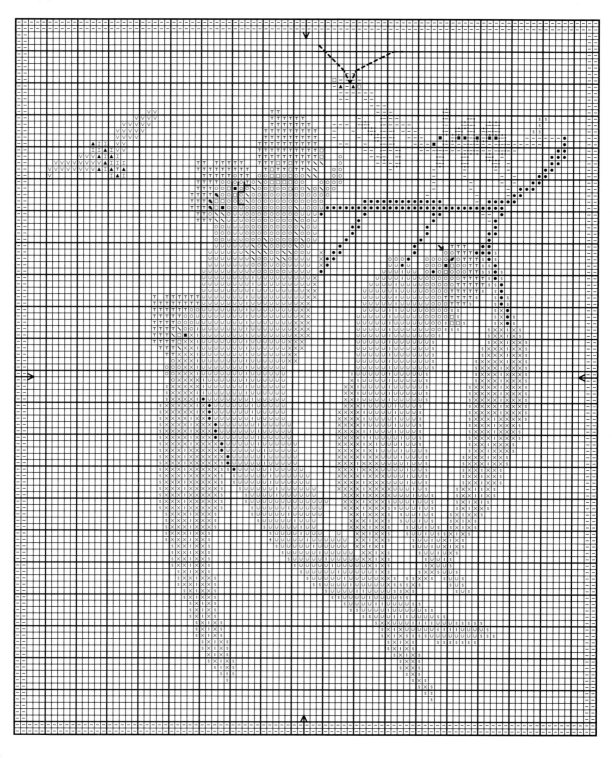

## KEY

| | | | | | | |
|---|---|---|---|---|---|---|
| ◹ | 7215 medium salmon pink | ⊍ | 7370 light tartan green | ˥ | 310 black (Art. 117) back stitch for antennae – use 2 strands |
| ⊡ | 7121 light peach flesh | ⊺ | 7491 very light rose beige | ∵ | 3042 mauve (Art. 117) back stitch for Mantis – use 3 strands |
| ◼ | 7802 baby blue | ⊡ | 7356 medium rose brown | ⌐ | 7215 medium pink back stitch for hands – use full thickness of wool |
| ⊤ | 7582 moss green | ⊻ | 7928 ultra very light grey green | ˥! | 3772 dark skin pink (Art. 117) for eyelashes – use 1 strand |
| ⊟ | ecru | ⊞ | 7504 light golden olive | | |
| ⊟ | 7264 mauve | ⊠ | 7500 very light mocha brown | | |
| ▲ | black | ◻ | 7491 very light rose beige for background | | |
| ⊠ | 7394 fern green | | | | |

# Gumleaves doorstop

## Materials

DMC Tapestry Wool (Art. 486) in the following colours and skein quantities:

| | | | |
|---|---|---|---|
| 7121 | 1 | 7400 | 1 |
| 7174 | 1 | 7424 | 1 |
| 7175 | 1 | 7472 | 1 |
| 7194 | 1 | 7739 | 1 |
| 7217 | 1 | 7870 | 3 |
| 7224 | 1 | 7853 | 1 |
| 7264 | 1 | 7950 | 1 |
| 7313 | 1 | black | 1 |
| 7392 | 2 | | |

DMC Tapestry Wool (Art. 487), 4 hanks ecru

DMC Stranded Cotton (Art. 117), 1 skein each 611, 3772 and black

Zweigart Tapestry Canvas (Art. 604–48), 50 x 40 cm

Tapestry needle, size 22

Embroidery scissors

Roller tapestry frame

30 x 20 cm medium-weight cotton fabric, ecru

Machine cotton to match

Brick or piece of heavy wood to fit the needlepoint (If using a brick it will have to be completely dry. It may need baking in the oven to dry it out thoroughly)

Polyester wadding

Strong thread or wool for lacing

Straw needle, size 3 or 4

Find the centre of the tapestry canvas and tack vertical and horizontal lines along the centres. Mount the long sides of the canvas onto the roller frame.

The centre of the canvas corresponds with the centre of the Chart. Start the needlepoint here. Work the design with Continental Stitch. Work the background in Basketweave Stitch, following the shape shown by the chart.

When the needlepoint is complete, work the Back Stitch details using two strands of stranded cotton.

Remove the canvas from the frame and block it.

Cut one or two pieces of polyester wadding to fit each side of the brick or wooden block. (If the wadding is thin cut two layers, if it is thick then one layer will do.) Oversew the pieces of wadding together by hand and place the doorstop form inside before stitching the last sides closed. Pin the side seams of the needlepoint together and slip it over the brick to check that it fits. Adjust if necessary. Machine stitch the side seams. Trim the seam allowances on the canvas. Turn the needlepoint right side out and slip it over the padded doorstop. Lace the opposite sides of the canvas together across the bottom of the doorstop with the strong thread or wool.

Press the ecru fabric and place it on the bottom of the doorstop with right side out. Turn under the raw edges so that the fabric fits the bottom of the doorstop and slip stitch the fabric into position, using a doubled length of ecru machine thread in the straw needle.

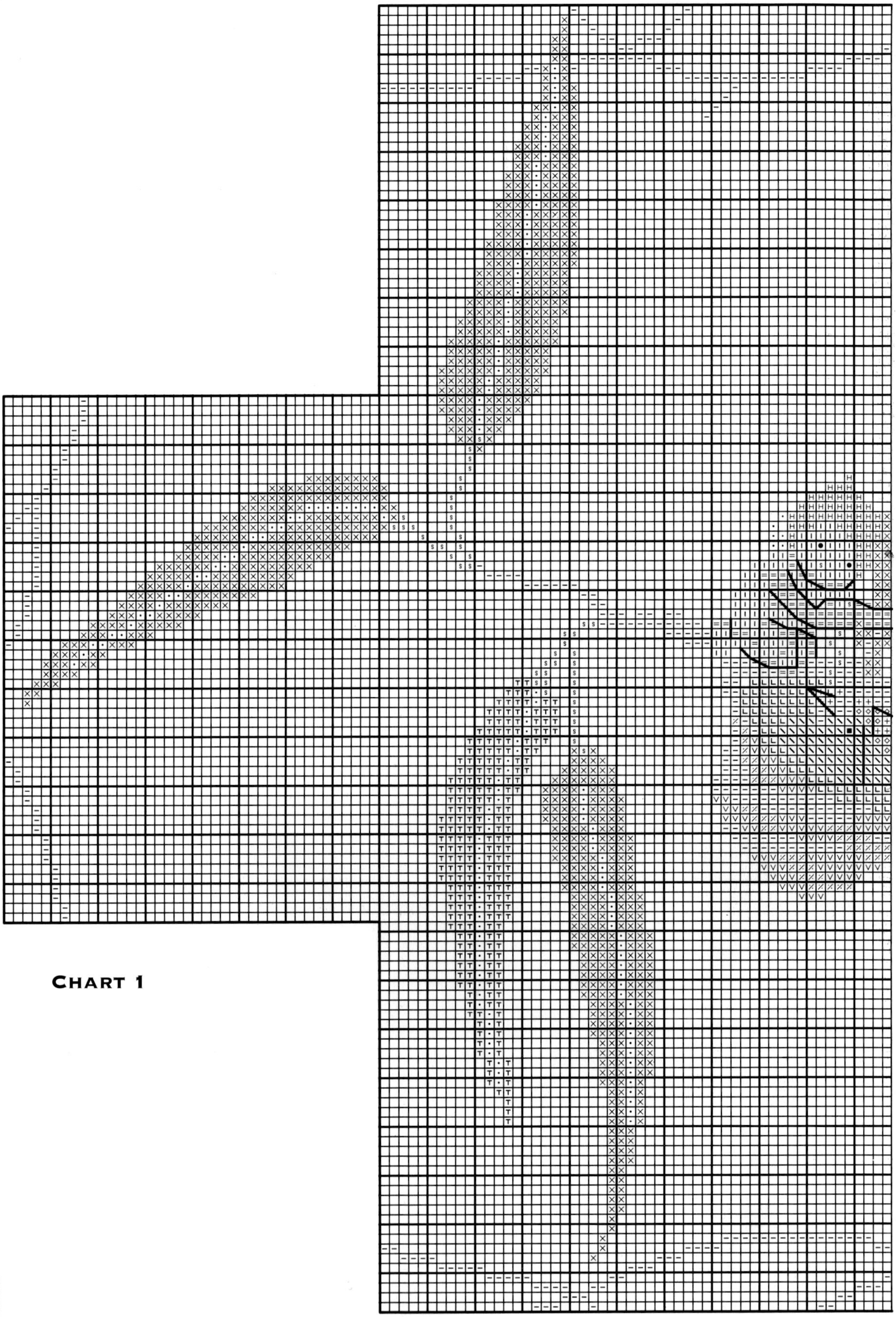

**CHART 1**

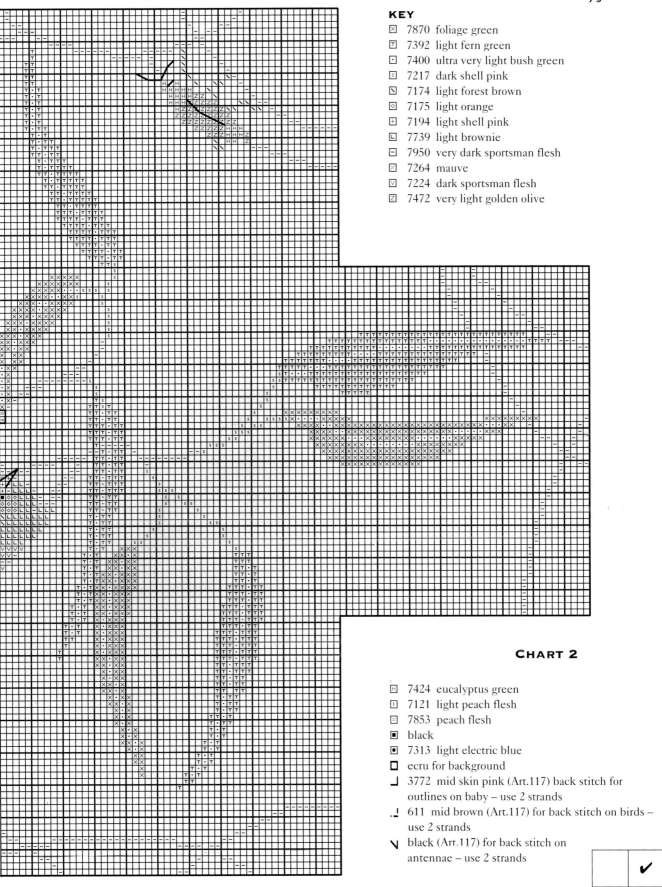

**KEY**

- ⊠ 7870 foliage green
- Ⓣ 7392 light fern green
- ⊡ 7400 ultra very light bush green
- ⊠ 7217 dark shell pink
- � 7174 light forest brown
- ⊠ 7175 light orange
- ⊞ 7194 light shell pink
- ⊔ 7739 light brownie
- ⊟ 7950 very dark sportsman flesh
- ⊠ 7264 mauve
- ⊻ 7224 dark sportsman flesh
- ☒ 7472 very light golden olive

**CHART 2**

- ⊞ 7424 eucalyptus green
- ⊡ 7121 light peach flesh
- ⊟ 7853 peach flesh
- ▣ black
- ◉ 7313 light electric blue
- ▢ ecru for background
- ◡ 3772 mid skin pink (Art.117) back stitch for outlines on baby – use 2 strands
- ◦ 611 mid brown (Art.117) for back stitch on birds – use 2 strands
- ◥ black (Art.117) for back stitch on antennae – use 2 strands

✔

The publisher has made every effort to ensure that all details were correct at time of printing.

**PROJECT MANAGER**
Kate Tully

**STYLIST**
Louise Owens

**PHOTOGRAPHER**
Andrew Elton

**STITCHERS**
June Bracken, Marj Clark, Nancy Copas, Fay Kelly, Georgina McCarthy, Jim Marshall, Lettie Marshall, Wendy Rinaldi, Mary Snepp, Kerry Stibbe, Fay Woolnough

**CHARTS**
David Marsh and John Snepp

**ACKNOWLEDGEMENTS**
DMC threads and Zweigart canvas
DMC Needlecraft Pty Ltd
51–55 Carrington Road
Marrickville NSW 2204

FolkArt paints and glaze
Myart — as for DMC Needlecraft Pty Ltd

Rambling Flowers Framing
Essex Framing Company
Rear 67 Grandview Street
Pymble NSW 2073

**STOCKISTS**
Linen and Lace of Balmain
213 Darling Street
Balmain NSW 2041
Telephone (02) 810 0719

Lisa Milasas
300 Sylvania Road
Gymea NSW 2227
Telephone 018 166 087

Victoria's Old Charm Antiques
82 Sydney Street
Willoughby NSW 2068
Telephone (02) 419 7008

Wardlaw
For your nearest stockist telephone (02) 660 6266

A BAY BOOKS PUBLICATION
First published in Australia in 1994 by Bay Books

An imprint of HarperCollins*Publishers*
25 Ryde Road, Pymble NSW 2073, Australia
31 View Road, Glenfield, Auckland 10, New Zealand

National Library of Australia Card Number and Cataloguing in Publication data:
Snepp, Alison
   May Gibbs Needlepoint
   ISBN 1 86378 053 X
   1. Canvas embroidery – Patterns. I. Gibbs, May, 1877-1969.
   II. Tully, Kate. III. Title.
746.442041

Printed in Australia by Griffin Press, Adelaide.

5 4 3 2 1
98 97 96 95 94